LifeLight

"In Him was life, and that life was the light of men." John 1:4

Acts, Part 2

LEADERS GUIDE

CONCORDIA PUBLISHING HOUSE • SAINT LOUIS

Priscilla pulled taut each stitch along the edge of the tent. She worked the bone needle through the rough goat's-hair cloth again and again. As she sewed, she thought about the challenges her family faced in their new home. Because her husband was Jewish, they were expelled from Rome (Acts 18:3). Because they were Christians, they were not welcome at the synagogue in Corinth (Acts 18:5–7). "It's like life for the children of Israel in the wilderness," she thought. "Always wandering; life in a tent; awaiting the Promised Land."

Earl H. Gaulke, editor

Revised from material prepared by Erwin Kolb and Paul Maier

This publication may be available in Braille, in large print, or on cassette tape for the visually impaired. Please allow 8 to 12 weeks for delivery. Write to Lutheran Braille Workers, P.O. Box 5000, Yucaipa, CA 92399; call toll-free 1-800-925-6092; or visit the website: LBWinc.org.

Cover illustration: Chris Ellison

Manufactured in the U.S.A.

7 8 9 10 11 12 13 14 15 32 31 30 29 28 27 26 25 24

Contents

Introduction

Welcome to LifeLight

A special pleasure is in store for you. You will be instrumental in leading your brothers and sisters in Christ closer to Him who is our life and light (John 1:4). You will have the pleasure of seeing fellow Christians discover new insights and rediscover old ones as they open the Scriptures and dig deep into them, perhaps deeper than they have ever dug before. More than that, you will have the pleasure of sharing in this wonderful study.

LifeLight—An In-depth Study

LifeLight is a series of in-depth Bible studies. The goal of LifeLight is that through a regular program of in-depth personal and group study of Scripture, more and more Christian adults may grow in their personal faith in Jesus Christ, enjoy fellowship with the members of His body, and reach out in love to others in witness and service.

In-depth means that this Bible study includes the following four components: individual daily home study; discussion in a small group; a lecture presentation on the Scripture portion under study; and an enhancement of the week's material (through reading the enrichment magazine).

LifeLight Participants

LifeLight participants are adults who desire a deeper study of the Scriptures than is available in the typical Sunday morning adult Bible class. (Mid-to-older teens might also be LifeLight participants.) While LifeLight does not assume an existing knowledge of the Bible or special experience or skills in Bible study, it does assume a level of commitment that will bring participants to each of the nine weekly assemblies having read the assigned readings and attempted to answer the study questions. Daily reading and study will require from 15 to 30 minutes for the five days preceding the LifeLight assembly. The day following the assembly will be spent reviewing the previous week's study by going over the completed study leaflet and the enrichment magazine.

LifeLight Leadership

While the in-depth process used by LifeLight begins with individual study and cannot achieve its aims without this individual effort, it cannot be completed by individual study alone. Therefore, trained leaders are necessary. You fill one or perhaps more of the important roles described below.

The Director

This person oversees the LifeLight program in a local center (which may be a congregation or a center operated by several neighboring congregations). The director

- serves as the parish LifeLight overall coordinator and leader;
- coordinates the scheduling of the LifeLight program;
- orders materials;
- convenes LifeLight leadership team meetings;
- develops publicity materials;
- recruits participants;
- maintains records and budgeting;
- assigns, with the leadership team, participants to small discussion groups;
- makes arrangements for facilities;
- communicates outreach opportunities to small-group leaders and to congregational boards;
- follows up on participants who leave the program.

The Assistant Director *(optional)*

This person may assist the director. Duties listed for the director may be assigned to the assistant director as mutually agreeable.

The Lecture Leader

This person prepares and delivers the lecture at the weekly assembly. **(Lesson material for the lecture leader begins on p. 7.)** The lecture leader

- prepares and presents the Bible study lecture to the large group;
- prepares worship activities (devotional thought, hymn, prayer), using resources in the study leaflet and leaders guide and possibly other outside sources;
- helps the small-group discussion leaders to grow in understanding the content of the lessons;
- encourages prayer at weekly leadership team and discussion leaders meetings.

The Small-Group Coordinator *(optional; the director may fill this role)*

This person supervises and coordinates the work of the small-group discussion leaders. The small-group coordinator

- recruits with the leadership team the small-group discussion leaders;
- trains or arranges for training of the discussion leaders;
- assists the director and discussion leaders in follow-up and outreach;
- encourages the discussion leaders to contact absent group members;
- participates in the weekly leadership team and discussion leaders equipping meetings;
- provides ongoing training and support as needed.

The Small-Group Discussion Leaders

These people guide and facilitate discussion of LifeLight participants in the small groups. **(Lesson material for the small-group leaders begins on p. 55.)** There should be one discussion leader for every group of no more than 12 participants. The small-group discussion leaders are, perhaps, those individuals who are most important to the success of the program. They should, therefore, be chosen with special care and be equipped with skills needed to guide discussion and to foster a caring fellowship within the group. These discussion leaders

- prepare each week for the small-group discussion by using the study leaflet and small-group leaders guide section for that session;
- read the enrichment magazine as a study supplement;
- guide and facilitate discussion in their small group;
- encourage and assist the discussion group in prayer;
- foster fellowship and mutual care within the discussion group;
- attend weekly discussion leaders training meetings.

Leadership Training

LifeLight leaders will meet weekly to review the previous week's work and plan the coming week. At this session, leaders can address concerns and prepare for the coming session. LifeLight is a 1½-hour program with no possibility for it to be taught in the one hour typically available on Sunday mornings. Some congregations, however, may want to use the Sunday morning Bible study hour for LifeLight preparation and leadership training. In such a meeting, the lecture leader and/or small-group coordinator may lead the discussion leaders through the coming week's lesson, reserving 5 or 10 minutes for problem solving or other group concerns.

While it requires intense effort, LifeLight has proven to bring great benefit to LifeLight participants. The effort put into this program, both by leaders and by participants, will be rewarding and profitable.

The LifeLight Weekly Schedule

Here is how LifeLight will work week by week:

1. Before session 1, each participant will receive the study leaflet for session 1 and the enrichment magazine for the course. The study leaflet contains worship resources (for use both in individual daily study and at the opening of the following week's assembly) and readings and study questions for five days. Challenge questions will lead those participants who have the time and desire a greater challenge into even deeper levels of study.
2. After the five days of individual study at home, participants will gather for a weekly assembly of all LifeLight participants. The assembly will begin with a brief period of worship (5 minutes). Participants will then join their assigned small discussion groups (of 12 or fewer, who will remain the same throughout the course), where they will go over the week's

study questions together (55 minutes). Assembling together once again, participants will listen to a lecture presentation on the readings they have studied in the previous week and discussed in their small groups (20 minutes). After the lecture presentation, the director or another leader will distribute the study leaflet for the following week. Closing announcements and other necessary business may take another five minutes before dismissal.

In some places some small groups will not join the weekly assembly because of scheduling or other reasons. Such groups may meet at another time and place (perhaps in the home of one of the small group's members). A congregation may record the lecture given by the lecture leader at the weekly assembly and duplicate it for use by other groups meeting later in the week.

3. On the day following the assembly, participants will review the preceding week's work by rereading the study leaflet they completed (and that they perhaps supplemented or corrected during the discussion in their small group) and by reading appropriate articles in the enrichment magazine.

Then the LifeLight weekly study process will begin all over again!

Recommended Study Resources for Acts

The Lutheran Study Bible. St. Louis: Concordia Publishing House, 2009. This resource contains more than 26,000 study and application notes, a thorough reference guide, and more than 90,000 cross-references, as well as a 31,000-entry concordance, maps, charts, and timelines.

Lutheran Bible Companion. St. Louis: Concordia Publishing House, 2014. This new resource is a highly visual two-volume handbook that welcomes Christians to a deeper exploration of the cultural and historical contexts of the events captured in Scripture and the Apocrypha.

Reformation Heritage Bible Commentary: Acts. St. Louis: Concordia Publishing House, coming 2016. This new Bible commentary series is a powerful tool for those wanting to better understand the background information on authorship, history, settings, and themes of the Gospel. Features the ESV and KJV side by side with quotes from key reformers.

A Step toward World Evangelization (Paul's First Mission Journey)

Acts 13–14

Preparing for the Session

Central Focus

The Holy Spirit calls Paul and Barnabas to take the Gospel into Asia Minor, as the Gospel continues to move from Jerusalem to the ends of the earth.

Objectives

That participants, led by the Holy Spirit, will

1. possess a more complete understanding of how the Holy Spirit caused the Gospel to be spread from Jerusalem to the ends of the earth;
2. become more confident in their own witness of the Gospel to others;
3. be encouraged as they see and experience conflicts among "erring and faithful" Christians;
4. be better able to meet and respond to opposition to the Gospel;
5. praise God for the growth of the church.

Note for the small-group leaders: Lesson notes and other materials you will need begin on page 55.

Session Plan

Worship

Each week the study leaflet will suggest that participants experiment with a prayer posture. Encourage participants to use that posture each day as they study their lessons at home, and then open the large group session with the same posture. This week explain that folded hands can serve two purposes: It may simply keep our hands from doing other things so we can focus on our prayer. Or it may (also) serve as a symbol, either of helplessness or some other quality. This week participants are urged to think of the joined fingers as the union between the Vine and the branches.

Read John 15:1–8. Then read together the prayer from the study leaflet, or speak a prayer of your own. Introduce the hymn "God, Whose Almighty Word" by pointing to this phrase in stanza 1, "hear us, we humbly pray," and connecting it to the theme of Study 1.

Note: Concordia Publishing House has available *Every Voice a Song*, a 9-CD set of organ accompaniments for 180 hymns and liturgy. All the initial worship hymns in the LifeLight courses are included in this resource. It's especially helpful for mission congregations and small parishes. See the list of study resources on page 6.

Devotion (optional)

Has the thought ever crossed your mind that God wanted you to take the Gospel to someone? Perhaps this was or is someone near at hand—someone you know at work or a neighbor, an acquaintance, perhaps even someone in your own family. Has the thought ever crossed your mind that God wanted you to take the Gospel to someone like that?

God calls upon all Christians to witness to others, to share the Good News that God was reconciling the world to Himself in Christ, not counting our sins against us. We fulfill this calling right where we are—at our places of employment, in our neighborhoods, within our families. God gives us the power to make such a witness, and He uses and blesses the witness we give. While we often fail to give a clear witness, the Lord forgives us and gives us opportunities to try again.

All Christians are to be the Lord's witnesses where they are. But some Christians God calls to leave their surroundings to take the Gospel to people far away. In our lesson this week we read of how the Holy Spirit called Paul and Barnabas for this work. The Holy Spirit still calls such missionaries—those who are sent by God to far-off places with the Gospel. Those of us whom God has not called for this particular work still, however, have a part in their ministry. We support such missionaries with our prayers and with our gifts. We may be certain that the congregation at Antioch upheld Paul and Barnabas in their prayers all the while these two members of their church were absent doing the work for which the Holy Spirit had called them. We also will want to remember in our prayers those whom God has called to take the Gospel to every area of the world, and we will want to support them with our financial gifts through our congregation and church body. And as they fulfill their calling, we will fulfill our calling to be witnesses for Jesus in our own setting.

Lecture Presentation

Introduction

In the first half of the Book of Acts Luke reported the birth of the Christian church at Pentecost, the confrontations between priestly authorities in Jerusalem and the apostles, the stoning of Stephen, the persecution by Saul of Tarsus and his subsequent conversion, and Peter's mission activities in Palestine. The second half of Acts focuses in fascinating detail on the life, adventures, and ministry of the now-converted Saul, who would one day be called St. Paul. This is the stirring account of how a faith born in the hills of Judea would penetrate the imperial capital of Rome 1,500 miles away in an incredibly brief period of time.

1 The First Mission Target: Cyprus (13:1–12)

Antioch was the capital of Syria, the Roman province just north of Palestine, and it became a vigorous seedbed for a growing church. Both Jews and Gentiles were converted to Christianity, and it was here that Jesus' followers largely abandoned their bulky title, "Followers of the Way," and took on the name by which they would be known ever afterwards: "Christians" (11:26). One of the early leaders in the church at Antioch was Barnabas, a sturdy, imposing Jew from Cyprus who had helped introduce the converted Saul to the Christian leadership in Jerusalem (9:27).

Sensing the need for more church workers in Antioch, Barnabas took the road that wound around the northeastern corner of the Mediterranean to Tarsus, 80 miles away, where he found his friend Saul and returned with him to Antioch. This sets the stage for what would become the first specifically organized missionary expedition in church history, the first of the tours that aimed to plant the flag of the faith in the very heart of paganism in Asia Minor (present-day Turkey), then Greece, and finally Rome.

Verse 2—It was probably in A.D. 47 that the Spirit told praying believers in Antioch, "Set apart for me Barnabas and Saul for the work to which I have called them." They were selected from quite a field of candidates, including Manaen, a courtier and friend of Herod Antipas (the ruler of Galilee during the ministry of Jesus) who had converted to Christianity.

Verse 3—It was a trio that embarked on ship from the port of Seleucia near Antioch. Barnabas had invited his cousin, John Mark, to join the expedition. This was the future author of that brisk and probably earliest Gospel, Mark. Most likely they weighed anchor at the opening of the sailing season—about March 10—since strong westerlies blow later in the spring and their voyage would not have been so direct.

Verse 4—Their destination was Cyprus, the "Copper Island." The choice was hardly a mystery: this was Barnabas's homeland, where relatives were waiting to learn the Good News and where such personal contacts would assist the missionaries. Verses 5–6—Landing at the eastern port of Salamis, they traversed Cyprus until they reached Paphos on the west coast, the provincial capital of the island.

Verses 7–8—Cyprus was one of Rome's senatorial provinces, and at this time it was governed by a proconsul named Sergius Paulus. He himself met Barnabas, Saul, and John Mark and inquired about their mission. It was Saul who took the initiative, giving so eloquent a response that the Roman was quite impressed. But the governor, like many heads of state, also had clients, opportunists, and hangers-on at his headquarters, and one of them was a magician or sorcerer named Bar-Jesus. Worried that his influence over the governor might slip if he converted to Christianity, Bar-Jesus opposed Saul.

Verses 9–10—"You are a child of the devil!" snapped Saul, in some of the strongest language recorded from his lips. "Will you never stop perverting the right ways of the Lord?" The apostle was angry for two reasons: (1) Bar-Jesus (or Elymas, his Greek name) was interrupting what would possibly be Saul's first major Gentile conversion, at least the first we know of; and (2) as a Jew,

Bar-Jesus should not have been dabbling in the occult, especially since his name, meaning "son of Jesus," could further have confused the governor, who was inquiring about Jesus, the Christ.

Verses 11–12—This man was a hindrance on all counts! Small wonder that God, through Saul, struck him with blindness, however temporary. This was the first recorded miracle from the hand of Saul, and it so impressed Sergius Paulus that he believed the apostolic message—a strategic conversion of a genuine historical personality. An inscription in Rome shows that L. Sergius Paulus was formerly a flood-control commissioner in that city.

In reporting this episode Luke inserts his famous shift in referring to the apostle by name in verse 9: "Then Saul, who was also called Paul." And Paul he would be called from here on. "Paulus" was a similar-sounding name among Greeks and Romans, the targets of his mission.

2 Proclaiming the Good News in Pisidian Antioch (13:13–52)

Having accomplished their mission in Cyprus for the present, Paul, Barnabas, and John Mark took a ship from Paphos and sailed northwest to Perga on the southern coast of Asia Minor. Verse 13—There, however, the missionaries suffered a personal crisis: Young John Mark suddenly abandoned his colleagues and returned to Jerusalem—why is not stated in the New Testament. Was John Mark ill? homesick? indecisive? a tenderfoot? a slacker?

Very likely it was something else. When the trio had left Antioch, Barnabas was clearly in charge of the expedition as Paul's original mentor. Yet, by the time they reached Cyprus, Paul had clearly taken over leadership of their mission tour. John Mark, as Barnabas's cousin, may have resented what he thought to be a takeover of leadership by an "outsider" from such "insiders" as themselves, who had been charter members of the church.

Whatever the reason for John Mark's defection, the apostles were obviously also human beings—a consolation for us today in any current church squabbles!

Verse 14—The initial goal of Paul and Barnabas's thrust into Asia Minor was another city named Antioch, a hundred miles inland. Pisidian Antioch was a very cosmopolitan community, with Galatian, Phrygian, Greek, Jewish, and Roman inhabitants. A large influx of veterans from the Roman army had also recently settled there. Of all these ethnic groups, however, Paul and Barnabas would first proclaim the Good News to their own kind—a standard procedure used by Paul from now until the end of the Book of Acts.

They went into the synagogue at Antioch on the Sabbath and sat down. Verse 15—After the standard two Scripture readings, from the Law and the Prophets, the rulers of the synagogue invited them to address the congregation. Verses 16–41—Paul stood up to deliver a sermonette that could not more effectively have linked Jesus to scriptural prophecy. Like the martyred Stephen, he skimmed the highlights of Israel's past (vv. 17–22), but when he reached King David he shifted directly to David's messianic descendant. Jesus, said Paul, was prosecuted by the Jerusalem authorities because they failed to see scriptural prophecies fulfilled in Jesus. But rejection and death were followed by resurrection and new life not only in the case of Jesus, but also for all who believed.

Verse 42—Paul's message about the Messiah who had finally arrived raised a sensation in the synagogue, and they were invited back for the next Sabbath. Verse 44—A week later, the word-of-mouth phenomenon had caused "almost the whole city" to turn out for the two missionaries.

Verses 45–47—This multitude, however, also included some representatives of Jewish orthodoxy who contradicted Paul's claims. After what must obviously have been a heated debate, Paul finally grasped what would become his ready alternative whenever he was confronted by Jewish rejection of the Christian message. Ominously, he warned, "We had to speak the word of God to you first. Since you reject it and do not consider yourselves worthy of eternal life, we now turn to the Gentiles. For this is what the Lord has commanded us: 'I have made you a light for the Gentiles, that you may bring salvation to the ends of the earth.'"

There were more than enough Gentiles for a mission field in Antioch, with its crazy-quilt of different ethnic groups. It is possible, in fact, that Paul and Barnabas had originally aimed for Antioch on the recommendation of Sergius Paulus, because archaeology has shown that the family of the governor of Cyprus had roots in that city. Verse 48—With only paganism as their religious foundation, the Gentiles of Antioch gave a positive response to the Christian message, and a congregation was founded there.

Verses 50–52—Unhappily, however, increasing pressures from the synagogue finally led to outright expulsion of the two missionaries. But before leaving Antioch, they had the satisfaction of seeing their new converts "filled with joy and with the Holy Spirit." The wonder of Pentecost was continuing.

3 On to Iconium and Lystra (14:1–20)

Verse 1—Paul and Barnabas now headed eastward to Iconium (called Konya in modern Turkey), a city well situated on a fertile fruit-and-grain-producing plain. Here they pursued a mission pattern parallel to what they had undertaken in Antioch, preaching first in the Jewish synagogue of the city. Verse 3—Supernatural signs and wonders only added to the effectiveness of their message, with the result that "a great number" of both Jews and Gentiles converted. Yet here again, orthodox Jews challenged their success, which divided the city. Verse 6—Lest they be mistreated and even stoned, the apostles fled Iconium for Lystra. They had, though, this powerful consolation: the second church in Asia Minor had been founded, and it would thrive.

Verses 8–10—Lystra lay 25 miles south-southwest of Iconium, but, although a sister city to Antioch in boasting a colony of Roman army veterans, it was clearly more rural and less sophisticated, if the next extraordinary scene is any indication. After Paul and Barnabas arrived in town, Paul used a great sign to add credibility to his great message. Fixing his gaze on one of his listeners, a cripple from birth, he cried, "Stand up on your feet!" The cripple did just that and began walking.

Verse 11—The phenomenon was too much for the crowd that had gathered. Abandoning the Greek in which they and Paul had been communicating, they shouted, in their native Lycaonian tongue, "The gods have come down to us in human form!" Verse 12—And such gods! Barnabas they hailed as Zeus, father of the gods and men in Greek mythology; while Paul, the chief spokesperson, they called Hermes, the god of communication.

Because of these names, scholars have long assumed that Barnabas must have had the more imposing figure of the two, with Paul smaller and more vocal. In fact, *paulus* is a Latin adjective meaning "small" or "little." But it was also a common proper name in several of the great families of Rome, whose bearers were anything but small. More convincing are the earliest portraits of Paul in the Roman catacombs, which often show him as a smallish figure with a pointed, gray beard.

The acclaim at Lystra was more than the sort of flattery given King Agrippa that fateful morning in Caesarea (12:21–23). Those were only words. Here the bedazzled pagans went on to action. The local priest of Zeus was so sure that the chief deity on Olympus had actually arrived in Lystra that he was preparing oxen and garlands to offer public sacrifice to the missionaries! Before we laugh at the naiveté of the Lystrans, it should be noted that it was in this area of the world that the famous Greek myth of Baucis and Philemon had its setting. Baucis and Philemon were an aged couple who one day supposedly offered hospitality to *Zeus and Hermes* as the two gods approached in the *likeness of men*, for which the couple's miserable cottage was transformed into a splendid temple. Would lightning strike twice in the same area?

Verses 14–17—Paul and Barnabas instantly put an end to such speculation. Tearing their garments at the sacrilege, Paul cried, "Why are you doing this? We too are only men, human like you. We are bringing you good news, telling you to turn from these worthless things to the living God," whom he went on to describe.

Verse 19—Was it chagrin at their blunder that made the crowd lend their ready ears to adversaries, Jews who had just made a trip from Antioch and Iconium to denounce the apostles? A drastic change of mood swept the multitude. The "gods" were now seen as impostors who had to be punished. Before his supporters could save him, Paul was stoned and then dragged outside the city by a shrieking mob, who left him there for dead.

Verse 20—Actually, Paul had doubtless been knocked unconscious by one of the stones. When Barnabas and the new believers of Lystra gathered anxiously around him, Paul regained his senses and stood up, bruised but not mortally injured.

Any thoughts of self-pity could hardly have cluttered his mind, for he would have been the first to recall a man named Stephen, and how he was here receiving a slight taste of his own medicine.

4 Derbe and the Return (14:21–28)

Verses 21–23—The next day they left for Derbe, the final town on their itinerary, about a day's journey eastward. Here they preached without incident and "won a large number of disciples," the first place in Galatia where they had not encountered a determined opposition. Paul would visit Derbe again on his second mission journey, and one of its residents, Gaius, became Paul's disciple and would accompany him on part of his third mission journey.

From Derbe it would have been easiest for Paul and Barnabas to continue eastward through the Taurus mountain pass and home to Antioch in Syria. But what was easiest was not always best for the Gospel. Since it was important to gauge the progress of the new missions they had founded, the two apostles went three times as far homeward in the opposite direction, bracing up the new believers in Lystra, Iconium, and Antioch, and appointing elders (pastors) to guide them. This prudent gesture led to permanent Christian churches in all these cities, some lasting until the time of the Turkish conquest in the fifteenth century.

Verses 26–28—The last three verses of Acts 14 show Luke's meticulous concern with geographic accuracy, adding places like Perga and Attalia to his record of the apostles' itinerary. All these sites have been identified today, and this adds compelling credibility to the entire account. Unlike almost all other religious systems, Christianity is based on hard fact, involving *real* people who lived and traveled in *real* places during a *real* segment of past history.

Upon reaching the Mediterranean coast, Paul and Barnabas caught a ship bound for Syria. When they finally returned to Antioch, they called the church together and gave what must have been an exciting and colorful mission report. It had not an ounce of self-credit or bragging, since God was given all the honor for having "opened the door of faith to the Gentiles."

Conclusion

Christianity's first crucial step toward world evangelization had now taken place. That step was bold, deliberate, and courageous. It had involved great effort, inconvenience, embarrassment, hazards, and sacrifice. Still, Paul and Barnabas had found joy in the process, since through prayer and implicit faith they had sought the Holy Spirit's guidance. God rewarded their venture with an eventual success that was extraordinary: Asia Minor became one of the strongest centers of Christianity in the critical first five centuries A.D. The conversion of the Mediterranean world was off to a splendid start.

Do one or two individuals make a difference? So often in life we tend to think that our one vote gets lost in an election, our local efforts to light a candle rather than curse the darkness are a futile gesture. At such times, we ought to remember Paul's first mission journey, and how a lonesome pair of apostles—two versus many thousands—began to change the world for the better, despite being hopelessly outnumbered. Individuals do count in God's sight! One person can change history!

Concluding Activities

Speak a brief prayer, asking God's blessing upon participants in this LifeLight course. Make any necessary announcements. Distribute study leaflet 2 and the enrichment magazine. Encourage participants to browse in the magazine and keep it as a helpful reference for coming lessons.

Encourage participants to set a weekly plan for their LifeLight study. A consistent daily schedule works best for most. Some begin or end the day with LifeLight. Others find another time during the day at home or during a break or lunch hour at work. Invite participants to share their practices, especially if your group has some who are new to LifeLight.

Agreeing That All Nations Are Included (The Apostolic Council of Jerusalem)

Acts 15

Preparing for the Session

Central Focus

The assembled leaders of the church affirm and declare the fundamental principle of the Gospel that salvation is through faith in Christ alone, without keeping the laws of the old covenant.

Objectives

That participants, led by the Holy Spirit, will

1. understand more clearly the Gospel principle that salvation is by faith in Christ alone, without the works of the Law;
2. become more confident of salvation through faith alone;
3. be unswayed by claims that they must do something besides trust in Christ to be saved;
4. in Christian freedom and love avoid offending those who are weaker in faith or who are still under the burden of erring consciences.

Note for the small-group leaders: Lesson notes and other materials you will need begin on page 58.

Session Plan

Worship

Comment on the prayer posture of holding hands while praying as a symbol of "agreeing together in prayer" and have the entire group hold hands as you read the Scripture (Matthew 18:19–20) and speak the prayer. Use either the prayer in the study leaflet or a prayer of your own. Do not ask the group to read since they need both hands to hold hands with others.

Continue with the hymn printed in the study leaflet. Accompaniments are available in denominational hymnals, such as *Lutheran Worship* (refer to hymnal index). Note: Concordia Publishing House has available *Every Voice a Song,* a 9-CD set of organ accompaniments for 180 hymns and liturgy. All the initial worship hymns in the LifeLight courses are included in this resource. It's especially helpful for mission congregations and small parishes. See the list of study resources on page 6.

Devotion (optional)

"You would think that a church would be the last place where there would be arguments and disagreements. In the church, of all places, you would expect to find harmony, mutual consideration, love, and peace."

Yes, you would. Until you remembered that the devil is trying his hardest to block and oppose the Gospel from doing its saving work. Until you remembered that the Gospel meets opposition as well as acceptance. Until you remembered that Christians are people who carry around throughout life on this earth their old sinful natures, as well as their new spiritual natures.

These considerations and others explain why the church is sometimes the scene of conflict and why forgiveness and reconciliation among Christians are sometimes necessary. Of course Christians strive for peace. They forgive one another when they are offended, and they are patient, bearing with one another. Christians avoid being contentious and argumentative. But there are times when Christians must resist the devil, contend for the faith, and even rebuke one another. There are times when love and harmony demand tenacity and toughness.

In our study this week we find such a situation. Finding such a situation, and others like it, in Scripture encourages us. We find that the Lord can and does see His church through conflict. We find that Christians can and do learn to forgive and reconcile. We find that we must sometimes stand up for the Gospel—sometimes for the sake of the very people we are opposing.

Lecture Presentation

Introduction

The most important church council ever held was not at Nicaea or Rome or Constantinople, but at Jerusalem—the event sandwiched in between Paul's first and second mission journeys. But for the decisions of that gathering, Christianity might have become (humanly speaking) nothing more than a splintered offshoot of Judaism, a tiny sect rather than the world's largest religious system, which outnumbers its mother Judaism by 100-to-1. The council debated this crucial question: Can Gentiles become Christians directly, or must they first become Jews? The rest of history hung on the answer.

1 How Does One Become a Christian? The Answer of the Judaizers (15:1–3)

A certain nostalgia for early Christianity and its rapid growth rate moves many believers today. If we could only get back to the dedication and vigor of the early church, they suggest, we could move mountains of indifference and win the world for Christ. Perhaps this is true. On the other hand, it is very easy to idealize the experiences of primitive Christianity, where all was hardly sweetness and light. Besides the spectacular extension of the church, Luke very candidly, very honestly also records the squabbles and quarreling that went on in early Christianity. (Incidentally, this also demonstrates the integrity and credibility of Luke as a historian, even if that was not his intention.)

After the sad affair of Ananias and Sapphira (Acts 5:1–11) and the complaining of the Jerusalem widows (6:1–6) came three shockers: (1) the bad, restrictive theology of Judaizing Christians that threatened to undermine everything Paul and Barnabas had accomplished; (2) the Paul versus Barnabas tiff in Antioch; and (3) the Paul versus Peter spat in the same city. First, the case of the Judaizers.

Among the Jerusalem Christians was a group of very strict interpreters of Jewish law—"the circumcision party" of Christian Pharisees who were later called Judaizers. A foretaste of their theology had surfaced when Peter returned from his mission to Cornelius, when they criticized him for dining with "uncircumcised men" (11:3). Though Peter's reply satisfied them for a time, the narrow-minded legalists now dispatched representatives to Antioch, who insisted that the only way a Gentile could become a Christian was to become a Jew first: 15:1—"Unless you are circumcised, according to the custom taught by Moses, you cannot be saved." Despite the coming of Christ, they taught, the Old Testament Law in its entirety still applied to Christians.

Paul and Barnabas opposed this notion vigorously. In their journey through Asia Minor they had not required that their Gentile converts be circumcised or that they observe all of Jewish law, since salvation was attainable only through faith in Christ, not by fulfilling the Law. Quite a debate raged in the Antioch church, since the Judaizers were calling Paul and Barnabas's whole mission enterprise into question.

Verse 2—The church at Antioch now sent Paul, Barnabas, and "some other believers" to Jerusalem to consult with the apostles on so basic an issue. These "other believers" included Titus, cited only in Galatians 2:1, who was one of Paul's Greek converts, most probably from Antioch, and he had not been circumcised. In other words, here was a walking, breathing test case on the theological question: Was Titus a true Christian as he was, or would he have to undergo the Jewish rite of circumcision first?

Verse 3—En route to Jerusalem, Paul, Barnabas, and Titus did not miss the opportunity of reporting to believers in Phoenicia and Samaria the exciting news that even Gentiles were being converted to Christianity. Looking at this event from our twenty-first-century Gentile church, we miss the drama in the missionaries' report today. If we understand a little about those days of Jewish exclusivism, however—when one rabbinical prayer ran: "I thank Thee, Lord, that I was not born a Gentile, an animal, or a woman"—we may better understand the sensation. Today it would be like our stunned reaction to news that former leaders of terrorism are turning to Christ.

2 How Does One Become a Christian? The Answers of Peter and Paul (15:4–12)

The meeting in Jerusalem was the first church council in Christian history, and its decision opened the way for Christianity to become a world religion, a universal faith. The highest authorities in the Jerusalem church at this time were the apostles and elders who had gathered to debate the issue, with James (the half brother of Jesus), Peter, and John as the leading three "pillars of the church."

Verse 4—Paul was warmly received by the Christian leadership, and opened by giving the assembly a sample of the sort of Gospel he and his colleagues had been preaching to the Gentiles, to make sure that he was not "running or had run my race in vain," as he put it in his own letter to the Galatians (2:2). If he had preached a faulty version of the faith, his 15 years of study and missionizing would have been utterly wasted. Verse 5—Paul's theology sat well with everyone but the Judaizers, who insisted adamantly, "The Gentiles must be circumcised and required to obey the law of Moses."

Verses 7–9—A drone of discussion greeted that opinion, until Simon Peter stood up and fully seconded Paul's theology. The forthright fisherman reminded the council of how God had elected the Gentiles also, as witnessed by his own special mission to Cornelius (Acts 10). Verses 10–11—"Now then," he summed up, "why do you try to test God by putting on the necks of the [Gentile] disciples a yoke that neither we nor our [ancestors] have been able to bear? No! We believe it is through the grace of our Lord Jesus that we are saved, just as they are." It was an astonishing admission: not even a good Jew could hope to fulfill the Law and find salvation in the process. Only divine grace could accomplish that.

Verse 12—During the resulting silence Paul and Barnabas reviewed how extraordinarily God had blessed their efforts in Asia Minor. Would He have given them the power to perform miracles there if they had been preaching a wrong gospel? Evidently, the Judaizers had no response to that argument. How, in fact, could they have responded? The logic was faultless.

3 How Does One Become a Christian? The Decision of James and the Council (15:13–34)

The person who apparently had the final authority at the conclave was James, Jesus' half brother. (Note his statement in verse 19: "It is *my* judgment, therefore ...") We wish we knew far more about James, since what we do know is most intriguing. In the Gospels, he is the first named among Jesus' four half brothers, but during Jesus' public ministry, he seems to have had qualms and concerns over Jesus' activities. However, Jesus' resurrection and special appearance to him (1 Corinthians 15:7) swept away all doubts and transformed James into the leader of the Jerusalem church. Later, he most probably wrote the epistle bearing his name, and we also know how he died, even though the New Testament does not tell us. Instead, the Jewish historian Josephus reports a confrontation between James and the Jewish Sanhedrin in A.D. 62 that bears a strong parallel to Good Friday: against the wishes of the Roman governor, James was stoned to death—another martyr for the faith. But this lay in the future.

Now, at least a dozen years earlier, James showed his leadership by bringing the Jerusalem council to a decision. He clearly sided with Peter, Paul, and Barnabas. Arming himself with Scripture, James announced that Peter's activities with the Gentiles corresponded well with prophecies by Amos (9:11–12), Jeremiah (12:15), and Isaiah (45:21). 15:19–20—He said, "It is my judgment, therefore, that we should not make it difficult for the Gentiles who are turning to God. Instead we should write to them, telling them to abstain from food polluted by idols, from sexual immorality, from the meat of strangled animals and from blood."

Paul's more liberal message, then, was God's message! His preaching was authentic. He had not "run in vain"! Titus would not have to be circumcised, and Gentiles could now convert directly to Christianity without going through a kind of Jewish halfway house. The fourfold restrictions—three dietary and one moral—were very mild tokens asked of the Gentiles so as not to offend their fellow Jewish Christians.

The Jerusalem council had clearly opted for salvation by God's grace through faith rather than salvation by Law, a momentous turn for the future of Christian theology. As Paul would later write to the new Christians in Galatia: "We did not give in to them [the Judaizers] for a moment, so that the truth of the Gospel might remain with you" (Galatians 2:5).

Verses 22–30—Paul's victory was confirmed by a letter that the elders of the Jerusalem church wrote to the Gentile congregation in Antioch and surrounding areas. It was delivered by two special prophetic emissaries—Judas Barsabbas and Silas—who accompanied

Paul and Barnabas on the trip back to Antioch and who testified in their behalf for the freedom of the Gospel. The letter specifically stated that the Judaizers had had no apostolic instructions to trouble the believers there (v. 24), and the Christians of Antioch could not have been happier. No change in their beliefs was necessary. The Gospel of God's free grace in Christ was Good News indeed.

4 An Apostolic Argument at Antioch (15:35–41)

Verse 35—Because of Paul's evident success with the Gentiles, an almost official division of labor had been agreed upon at the close of the Jerusalem conclave: James, Peter, and John would concentrate primarily on the Jewish Christians, whereas Paul and Barnabas would specialize in Gentile mission work (Galatians 2:9). This may help explain the unhappy scene that followed soon after the council ended. Even though the squabble between Peter and Paul at Antioch is not reported in Acts but in Galatians, it *did* take place at this time, so we should deal with it briefly.

Galatians 2:11–21 tells us that the Judaizers of Jerusalem, despite their enormous setback, still tried to advance their cause, and a party of them returned to Antioch. Peter happened to be paying a visit to the church at Antioch about the same time, and at first he had had no scruples about dining with the Gentile converts there. When the Judaizers showed up, however, he stopped his table fellowship with the Gentiles to forestall any criticism from these militant traditionalists. Peter's inconsistency, however, grew contagious, and soon even Barnabas and other Jewish Christians were also dining on a strictly kosher basis, leaving Gentile believers by themselves—and justifiably offended. Possibly Peter felt that his mission, now mainly to the circumcised, dictated such conduct, but it remains a sad misstep in an otherwise noble career, a throwback to the Simon Peter of pre-Pentecost days. Barnabas's conduct, following as it did the first mission journey, was even less defensible.

Paul quickly set Peter straight. "I opposed him to his face," Paul later wrote the Galatians (2:11). He told Peter, (Galatians 2:14) "You are a Jew, yet you live like a Gentile and not like a Jew. How is it, then, that you force Gentiles to follow Jewish customs?" The freedom of the Gospel was at stake, and Paul would not let Peter risk it or return to legalism.

Verses 36–37—Fast on the heels of this spat came the Barnabas-versus-Paul quarrel on whether or not John Mark should come along on the second mission journey they were now planning. Barnabas agreed that it was time to revisit the new churches in Asia Minor, but he wanted his cousin to accompany them. Verse 38—Paul, however, "did not think it wise to take him, because he had deserted them in Pamphylia and had not continued with them in the work." Was Paul being pigheaded? obstinate? Perhaps he was just being realistic: The kind of expeditions they were planning would demand total commitment and reliability.

Verse 39—Barnabas refused to back down, and it actually led to a split between the two apostles: "They had such a sharp disagreement that they parted company." The quarrel had doubtless been made worse by Barnabas's weakness in the face of the Judaizers at Antioch. In any case, Barnabas now took John Mark with him on a separate mission journey to Cyprus, while Paul chose a new partner, Silas, who had helped deliver the letter of decision from the Jerusalem council to the church in Antioch. And so God worked good from bad: The net result of this dispute was two missionary expeditions instead of one. In the future, Paul would continue to recognize Barnabas as a working apostle like himself (1 Corinthians 9:6), and, happily, he would even become reconciled with Mark in Rome (Colossians 4:10).

Nevertheless, these two famous apostolic squabbles—Paul versus Peter, and Paul versus Barnabas—are certainly extraordinary, and they used to bother some of the church fathers. Jerome, a fourth-century church scholar, for example, tried to explain away Peter's conduct in Antioch and Paul's response as play-acting to teach a lesson, but Augustine, another church scholar who lived at the same time, totally disagreed with Jerome—almost causing *another* round of church controversy on this matter!

Augustine was right: The quarrel *did* happen in fact, and it need not be explained away. There is something very refreshing about the realism and honesty in the reports of the two quarrels in Antioch. Saints are obviously sinners too, capable of failure and mistakes, and their story is ever so much more believable when it is told in full.

Most other biographies in the Greco-Roman world of that period are laced with flattery of their subjects, and so lose much credibility. The Bible, on the other hand, is the one religious book in ancient literature that admits its heroes are sinners too and then provides an up-front catalogue of the sins. So instead of glossing over such unhappy episodes, Acts and the Letters of Paul report them with honesty and detail.

Another reason for including such scenes in the record may have been to comfort future generations of Christians. If, in the warm afterglow of the first Pentecost, the early church, informed and inflamed as it was by the Holy Spirit, could *still* become a cockpit of controversy between faithful and erring, parties and ethnic groups, then there is some small consolation for later generations of Christians, which have done—and are doing—the same thing.

However, there is also a lesson from the first Christians on how to *solve* such controversies. The decision at the Jerusalem council involved several elements: (1) *A Face-to-Face Confrontation.* There was no whispering campaign, no rush to publish, no indirect attacks or misunderstandings, but an open exchange between reasonable people, not extremists. (2) *Listening.* Possibly the most important verse in Luke's report on the conclave is 15:12: "The whole assembly became silent as they listened ..." An honest effort was made by each side to hear the other side. (3) *A Scriptural Solution.* James based his decision on three prophets—Isaiah, Jeremiah, and Amos—whom he deemed mouthpieces of God.

Those who are involved in church controversies today—especially in the local congregation—might well look back to Christian origins for Christian solutions!

Conclusion

The Apostolic Council of Jerusalem had not hatched a fresh or novel idea in approving Gentile conversions directly into Christianity. It was not pressured by the obvious successes of Paul and Barnabas in this regard. Rather, it was Jesus Himself who had issued orders to His disciples to reach and teach all nations (Matthew 28:19). Paul and Barnabas had followed those orders exuberantly, but others failed to have that sort of apostolic vision. And so the Jerusalem council became necessary.

It was a crucial breather between the first and second mission journeys, when the all-important question of how to become a Christian was finally given a definite answer. That reply, under the guidance of God, drew a wider circle to take others in rather than a narrower circle to shut others out. And that was the decision that would lead to what became the most successful single happening in the history of this planet: the holy Christian church.

Now Paul and his associates could venture out again, knowing that the Gospel they had proclaimed and would continue to proclaim was apostolic and absolutely genuine.

Concluding Activities

Speak a brief prayer asking the Lord to guide the church through its controversies in our own day, with the result that the Gospel will continue to remain free to do its saving work. Then make any necessary announcements. Ask whether participants are enjoying the enrichment magazines. Distribute study leaflet 3.

The Gospel Is Received and Rejected (Paul's Second Mission Journey—Part 1)

Acts 16:1–17:15

Preparing for the Session

Central Focus

The Holy Spirit guided Paul and his missionary companions to take the Gospel to Europe, where it was gladly received by some and passionately rejected by others in Philippi, Thessalonica, and Berea.

Objectives

That participants, led by the Holy Spirit, will

1. understand that some receive the Gospel with a faith that is the gift and work of the Holy Spirit, while others reject the Gospel with an unbelief that is the product of their own sinful human nature;
2. be grateful that the Holy Spirit enabled them to receive and believe the Gospel;
3. courageously stand by the Gospel and tell the Good News to others.

Note for the small-group leaders: Lesson notes and other materials you will need begin on page 61.

For the Lecture Leader

If your setting allows it and you have a large map of the journeys of Paul available, it will be very helpful to point out on the map the places you will talk about in your lecture presentation.

Session Plan

Worship

Have the entire group sit on their hands as you read the Scripture and the prayer in the study leaflet, or speak your own prayer. You may want to introduce the hymn as one of the finest hymns of trust in our hymnody and point to phrases like "Faith's strong hand the rock has found, Grasped it, and will leave it never" (stanza 3) or "As you now still wait to rise, Fix your hearts beyond the skies" (stanza 4).

Note: Concordia Publishing House has available *Every Voice a Song,* a 9-CD set of organ accompaniments for 180 hymns and liturgy. All the initial worship hymns in the LifeLight courses are included in this resource. It's especially helpful for mission congregations and small parishes. See the list of study resources on page 6.

Devotion (optional)

"When you're down, look up!"

Perhaps you have heard that bit of advice, or something like it. The Lord invites us to "call upon Me in the day of trouble; I will deliver you, and you will honor Me" (Psalm 50:15). It is a promise that the Lord repeats in Psalm 91:15 and again in Jeremiah 29:12.

In our reading this week we found Paul and Silas locked up tight, their legs secured in torturous pain in stocks, deep in a dungeon at Philippi. They did not deserve to be there, since they were innocent of the charges that brought them to that terrible and terrifying place. They had not received a fair trial. But they sang! Confined in that jail they sang hymns to God! And the Lord certainly delivered them—with a powerful earthquake that released them from their chains and threw open the doors of the prison.

But these servants of Christ were not the only ones delivered in that Philippian jail. The jailer himself was delivered that night! He and his household were delivered from sin and death and the power of the devil when Paul and Silas spoke the Gospel, the Good News of God's forgiveness and grace for Jesus' sake, to them. And this deliverance of the jailer and his household was even more wonderful than the deliverance of the brave missionaries from their troubles.

Thank God, we have been delivered too! We also have received the liberation that comes from God's grace. You probably were not delivered in a jail. But you were delivered, no matter where it happened, and in the wonderful freedom of the Gospel you remain and will remain forever. Thank God that He has delivered us from the worst trouble of all—confinement by sin and death, with the devil as our jailer!

Lecture Presentation

Introduction

Paul and Silas had not necessarily planned it that way, but the second mission journey would turn into a major campaign, a journey of many months that penetrated a new continent for Christ—Europe—and culminated in the cultural capital of Greece—Athens—as well as the Roman political capital—Corinth. As elsewhere, the Good News would be both joyfully received and passionately rejected.

It is no accident that Luke reported the second mission journey in such exciting and colorful detail in the Book of Acts. He himself was an eyewitness to much of it, evidently coming on board the tour at Troas in Asia Minor. From that point on, he would accompany Paul through many of his subsequent journeys.

1 Through Asia Minor to Macedonia (16:1–15)

Paul and his new companion, Silas, went overland this time, heading north and then westward around the corner of the Mediterranean to Asia Minor. Doubtless they visited Tarsus in Cilicia, Paul's hometown, where they may have stayed with relatives, and then set out across the formidable Taurus Mountains through a famous pass, the Cilician Gates. Famous conquerors, including Xerxes, Cyrus, Xenophon, and Alexander the Great, had all passed through the Gates, but now a solitary pair of missionaries were using the same pass for a spiritual conquest that would have far more permanent results.

Once on the higher Anatolian Plateau on the other side of the Cilician Gates, Paul and Silas stopped at the four Galatian cities that Paul had missionized some months earlier and delivered to them the decision of the Jerusalem Council to put no qualifications in the way of Gentile converts except for a few mild requests. Verses 1–2—At Lystra Paul was so impressed with a young man named Timothy, who enjoyed an excellent reputation among the Christians of the area, that he invited him to accompany them as co-worker.

Verse 3—With a Jewish mother and a Greek father, Timothy was a living symbol of the universality of the faith, and he gladly accepted. Unlike Titus, another young man who became Paul's co-worker somewhat later, Paul had Timothy circumcised. This may seem inconsistent, but was not: with a Jewish mother, Timothy was considered a Jew in Jewish law. Titus, on the other hand, was a Gentile. Timothy's circumcision would also gain easier acceptance among the Jews for himself and his message. (Incidentally, the rule that a person is deemed Jewish if born to a Jewish mother—regardless of the father—remains in force to the present day.)

Verse 6—After moving on to Iconium and Antioch, Paul, Silas, and Timothy intended to pass into the Roman province of Asia—roughly the western third of what is today's Turkey. Instead, the trio found themselves heading northwestward, "having been kept by the Holy Spirit from preaching the word in the province of Asia." This passage has knitted many Christian brows, but it does not mean that God was playing favorites with the Gospel. Rather, it was all a matter of timing: Paul would spend many months in Asia and its chief city, Ephesus, on the third mission journey. Now, however, the continent of Europe was waiting for their message.

Verse 9—Upon reaching the coast at Troas, very near the site of ancient Troy at the mouth of the Dardanelles, Paul had a vision during the night—most probably a dream—in which a man of Macedonia pleaded, "Come over to Macedonia and help us." Dreams carried far more significance in the ancient world than today, and the Bible records repeated instances where they served as a vehicle for communication between God and people.

Verse 10—"We got ready at once to leave for Macedonia," writes Luke, "concluding that God had called us to preach the gospel to them." Here is the celebrated "we" passage, in which Luke shifts from the third person, leading to the conclusion that he had joined the missionary threesome at Troas. What Luke was doing there, where his home was, and other background details are not known, but that Greek Gentile physician, now a missionary and later an author, would make immeasurable contributions to Christianity.

Verse 11—The four sailed to Macedonia by way of the island of Samothrace (which gave the art world the great "Winged Victory" statue), and the next day they reached the port of Neapolis—"New City" in Greek, the same term behind the name of the Italian city Naples. This was Paul's first step onto the continent of Europe.

Verse 12—Paul's objective was an important city of the area, Philippi—named for Philip of Macedon, father of Alexander the Great—which lay nine miles inland across a steep mountain ridge. From the top of this rise they easily saw Philippi lying at the spur of another hill and intercepting the Via Egnatia, the Roman highway running from Europe to Asia. And just west of the city they could view the broad plain on which, 93 years earlier, the armies of Antony and Octavian had vanquished those of Brutus and Cassius in avenging Caesar's assassination.

Verse 13—Paul and his associates broke their usual pattern at Philippi. Since apparently there was no Jewish synagogue there, they waited until the Sabbath and then went outside the city walls to the banks of the Gangites River about a mile west of Philippi, where there was supposed to be a gathering place for Jewish worship.

Verse 14—A group of pious women did meet there, among them a wealthy businesswoman named Lydia, who may have been either a Jewess or someone interested in Judaism. Lydia sold purple fabrics. The Phoenician "patent" on dyeing textiles in the simmering glands of the purple sea snail had now lapsed, and Asia Minor had also learned the secret of producing garments of royal purple that never faded. Lydia regularly imported these into Philippi and had a thriving business. Verse 15—Paul's preaching at the riverside chapel won her over to Christianity, and she asked for Baptism. Lydia was Paul's first convert in Europe, and her household quickly joined her in the faith. She even prevailed on the four missionaries to use her home as the base for their ministry at Philippi, and they gladly accepted.

2 In Prison at Philippi (16:16–40)

A very strange confrontation thrust the apostles into public attention in the city. Verses 16–17—As they were going to the riverside one day, a slave girl who was a fortune-teller pursued Paul and his colleagues, crying out, "These men are servants of the Most High God, who are telling you the way to be saved." The claim was accurate enough, but coming from a gypsy sort who profited from fortune-telling, it could hardly help the Christian cause.

Verse 18—Paul ignored the girl, but the scene was repeated for days on end, until Paul lost his patience and told the spirit inside the girl, "In the name of Jesus Christ I command you to come out of her!" The girl immediately returned to normal—joy for her, but grief for the shabby syndicate of her owners, who were profiting from the girl's supernatural abilities.

Verses 19–21—Seizing Paul and Silas, they dragged them into the central marketplace and indicted them before the city magistrates. "These men are Jews," said their spokesman, "and are throwing our city into an uproar by advocating customs unlawful for us Romans to accept or practice."

Romans? "Macedonian Greeks" might have been more accurate, but Philippi, like Antioch and Lystra, also had the status of a Roman colony. And since Jews were not supposed to make converts of Roman citizens, the girl's exploiters seized on this as a convenient charge against the missionaries.

Verses 22–23—But now the always-present crowds downtown joined in attacking Paul and Silas, and the city magistrates ordered them stripped and beaten with rods. This was against every standard of Greco-Roman justice: They had not bothered to hear a defense from the pair, probably assuming that where there was smoke, there must be fire. Evidently Timothy and Luke were not with their colleagues when the girl was healed, and whether they arrived at the marketplace in time to see them "severely flogged" is not known.

Verses 24–25—Paul and Silas were thrown into the city prison, where the jailer consigned them to an inner cell and anchored their feet in stocks—part security and part torture, since the wooden frame forced their legs apart in a cramped position. Rather than bemoan their condition, however, Paul and Silas prayed and sang cheerful hymns until midnight. Surprisingly, the other prisoners "were listening to them" instead of yelling derisive catcalls or obscenities.

Verses 26–27—Suddenly, a severe earthquake shook the foundations of the jail, tearing the prisoners' chains from their sockets and flinging open the doors to their cells. Perhaps the jailer had been in his office dozing through all the singing, but he could hardly sleep through an earthquake! No sight was more horrifying for a warden in ancient times than open doors in an empty prison. Since death was the usual punishment for such laxity, the desperate jailer drew out his sword and opted for suicide. According to Greco-Roman law, his widow could then inherit his estate without penalty, since her dead husband had served as his own judge, jury, and executioner, thus saving the state money.

Verses 28–30—"Don't harm yourself! We are all here!" Paul shouted from the murky depths of the dungeon. "Torches!" the jailer cried, and when light was brought, he rushed inside his prison and found it just as Paul had said. Falling down before them, he cried, "Sirs, what must I do to be saved?" One may think the jailer's question just a little too pat, too abrupt for such a situation. Probably, however, the man already had some knowledge of the sort of message Paul and Silas were bringing to Philippi. He had heard them testify to the Gospel as they sang and prayed! Verse 31—Paul replied with the Gospel-in-a-sentence: "Believe in the Lord Jesus, and you will be saved—you and your household."

Verses 32–34—The jailer brought Paul and Silas out of prison and into his own quarters, where he washed their wounds and fed them while Paul expanded on his original statement. Before the night was over, the elated jailer and his whole family had been baptized.

Verses 35–37—The next morning the city magistrates, with uneasy consciences, sent some police over with orders to release the missionaries. But Paul would have none of that. Bristling with injured innocence, he replied, "They beat us publicly without a trial, even though we are Roman citizens, and threw us into prison. And now do they want to get rid of us quietly? No! Let them come themselves and escort us out."

Verses 38–39—Paul was not being difficult. He had his good name to clear in Philippi so that the Good News might not have its validity impugned. The city magistrates, however, trembled at the news. Paul had them on three counts of miscarrying justice, and the worst, certainly, was the fact that Roman citizens were not to be beaten. One can almost see the town fathers falling all over themselves as they personally arrived to apologize to Paul and Silas and give them V.I.P. treatment while escorting them out of prison.

Verse 40—Paul and his associates paid a final visit to the new congregation meeting at Lydia's house, and then they departed after what must have been a tender good-bye. Paul would treasure the special bond he had with the believers in Philippi, and no congregation supported him in the future with more genuine love, prayers, and gifts than the Philippians, as Paul's later letter to them would show. Perhaps Luke had a hand in this, since he seems to have remained at Philippi for the next months in order to serve the new Christians there.

3 The Tumult in Thessalonica (17:1–9)

Verses 1–4—The Roman highway Via Egnatia led Paul, Silas, and Timothy westward to Amphipolis and Apollonia—well-known classical sites—and on to their next target city, Thessalonica. Although he would come to be called "the Apostle to the Gentiles," Paul began his ministry at Thessalonica in the synagogue, as he did wherever possible. Christianity, after all, rested on Jewish foundations and called itself "the new Israel," so this was the logical place to start. For three weeks he debated Scripture in the synagogue, showing how well Jesus fulfilled Old Testament prophecy. Some of the Jews were persuaded, including a hospitable sort named Jason, who threw open his home to the apostles. Certain prominent Greeks of Thessalonica also joined the fledgling congregation. Meanwhile, though, Paul and his co-workers had to do some serious tentmaking in order to support themselves here, according to 1 Thessalonians 2:9.

Verses 5–7—One day, while the missionaries were away, an angry crowd, fired up by opponents in the synagogue, stormed into Jason's house looking for Paul. Unable to find him, they grabbed Jason and several other believers instead, hauling them before the city magistrates with the indictment, "These men who have caused trouble all over the world have now come here," a phrase providing unintentional but dramatic testimony to the spread of the faith! "And Jason," they continued, "has welcomed them into his house. They are all defying Caesar's decrees, saying that there is another king, one called Jesus."

Verses 8–9—Pontius Pilate would have recognized the last charge, and it proved disturbing enough for the civic leaders. But Jason and the other Christians posted a peace bond and were released. Rather than embarrass their host further, the missionaries slipped away by night and traveled on to Berea. The church in Jason's house flourished, however, and this is the core congregation that had the honor of receiving the first two documents ever written in what would later be called the New Testament, namely, 1 and 2 Thessalonians. Jason himself would later join Paul in Corinth (Romans 16:21). Here was another man marked by the Gospel, and appropriately so, since Greek Jews generally chose the name Jason in Greek for their Semitic names, Joshua or Jesus.

4 A Welcome in Berea (17:10–15)

Verses 10–11—About 50 miles to the west-southwest lay Berea (today called Verria), and the synagogue there gave Paul a much better hearing, since "the Bereans were of more noble character than the Thessalonians, for they ... examined the Scriptures every day to see if what Paul said was true." No passage in the New Testament better demonstrates how important it was for earliest Christian preaching that Jesus' person and work be proclaimed as the fulfillment of Old Testament prophecy. For that reason, the first creed of the church was simply "Jesus Christ," which means "Jesus is the Messiah," the one to whom the Scriptures (i.e., the Old Testament) point.

Verse 12—Many in this Berean Bible class came to the faith, including "a number of prominent Greek women and many Greek men." As in his Gospel, Luke is always careful to include the crucial role of women in the life of Jesus and the birth of the church.

Verses 13–15—But the apostolic visit was again cut short by Jewish agitators who now arrived from Thessalonica to stir up a riot against the missionaries. In the eastern Mediterranean there was always an idle but reliable rabble in each town for such purposes—dry kindling just waiting to be set aflame. One good, decent riot was better than days of boredom! Paul was quickly smuggled out of Berea and onto a ship bound for Athens, while Silas and Timothy may have fronted for him by staying a while longer in Berea. The strategy worked.

Now another congregation had been founded in Macedonia, and it too would prosper. And so Macedonia, the homeland of Alexander the Great, became the first European country to hear the Good News from Paul. As has happened ever since, the message about Christ was both received and rejected. To say that the Gentiles received the faith while the Jews rejected it is simply not true. Many Jews believed while many Gentiles spurned it. Still, a pattern of greater reception among Gentiles than Jews was beginning to form.

Conclusion

We can learn much about how to spread the faith from this first European landfall of Paul and his associates. Their persistence and bravery in the face of violent opposition may put our efforts to shame, but what examples they set! Perhaps, too, we can take a lesson from their flexibility when confronted by a change of plans: They aimed for Ephesus but landed at Philippi, and yet surely made the best of it. We also should learn to adapt to circumstance and trust God's will for our lives.

It is also important for us to remember that the Acts account is not just "sacred" history but real history, and nothing shows this to better advantage than the second mission journey. Luke's care in showering his account with the names of towns and cities makes it easy to retrace the steps of the apostles today. All sites mentioned en route have been located, and many have even been excavated.

The ruins at Philippi are particularly impressive. Fortunately, there is no modern city to obliterate its ancient predecessor, which means that the excavations there show the very streets and foundations of Paul's day. The central marketplace or civic center where Paul and Silas were beaten is plainly visible, and it borders the Via Egnatia, the Roman highway over which the missionaries traveled. And in the eastern sector of the ruins, a sign in Greek hangs across the entrance to what looks like a large cavern. It translates, "The traditional prison of the Apostle Paul."

Such links between archaeology and Acts grow even stronger as we follow Paul, Silas, and Timothy to Athens and Corinth—the second part of the second mission journey, which focuses on the heart of Greece.

Concluding Activities

Speak a brief prayer, perhaps thanking God for the way in which the Gospel reached the individuals in your LifeLight group. Make any necessary announcements, and distribute study leaflet 4.

Getting the Message Straight (Paul's Second Mission Journey—Part 2)

Acts 17:16–18:22

Preparing for the Session

Central Focus

Paul directly confronts Greek paganism in Athens, where he presents the Gospel to people who do not know the true God, and he confronts once again the opposition of Jews in Corinth.

Objectives

That participants, led by the Holy Spirit, will

1. understand better both the difference between the Gospel and all other systems of belief and the points of contact between the Gospel and other systems of belief;
2. desire to prepare themselves for opportunities to present the Gospel to unbelievers;
3. become more effective witnesses of the Gospel;
4. value and utilize the partnership of fellow Christians in the task of presenting the Gospel to the world.

Note for the small-group leaders: Lesson notes and other materials you will need begin on page 64.

For the Lecture Leader

If possible, refer to a large map of the Mediterranean world at Paul's time as you make your lecture presentation.

Session Plan

Worship

Repeat the suggested posture of prayer as outlined in the participants' study assignment, using the one-way sign and the Scripture verses. You might want to demonstrate that you can point with the index finger to God and, by extending the thumb, point to yourself at the same time. Faith is always a personal relationship between one person and Jesus, between me and Jesus. So we say in the hymn "Jesus, Your blood and righteousness *My* beauty are, *my* glorious dress." Use the prayer in the study leaflet or speak a prayer of your own.

Continue with the hymn printed in the study leaflets. Accompaniments are available in denominational hymnals, such as *Lutheran Worship* (refer to hymnal index). Note: Concordia Publishing House has available *Every Voice a Song,* a 9-CD set of organ accompaniments for 180 hymns and liturgy. All the initial worship hymns in the LifeLight courses are included in this resource. It's especially helpful for mission congregations and small parishes. See the list of study resources on page 6.

Devotion (optional)

Have you ever found yourself surrounded by people who seemed to be completely different from you, who seemed to share none of the values you held?

Perhaps so. You may have traveled to an area of the world where the culture was greatly different from your own. Or a business or social situation may have placed you among people whose orientation to life seemed vastly different from your own.

In such situations, perhaps, we can better understand Paul's feelings as he, a Jew from the eastern Mediterranean world, strolled through the heart of Greek paganism in the great city of Athens. Even the ruins of this sophisticated civilization are a sight that still impresses today. But Paul, who saw the monuments of this civilization in their flowering, found the sight depressing.

He viewed the many temples and altars with great distress. Still, however, Paul addressed the adherents of these distressing objects with tact, seeking points of entry for the Gospel that was so opposite to the religions he found on display in Athens.

We can learn a lot from Paul in this situation. We can learn to be distressed, too, as we view the deplorable spiritual condition displayed in our own world. But we can learn to address the unbelievers who surround us also with tact, looking for points of entry for the Gospel. And when we find those points of entry, we can present the Gospel in a way that is likely to make the most headway. This is not minimizing or changing the Gospel but finding those places where the Gospel will make the greatest impact and will be seen most clearly for the dramatic and unique message that it is.

Lecture Presentation

Introduction

With Paul's arrival at Athens and Corinth, Christianity had moved out of the backwaters of the Mediterranean into the mainstream of the ancient world. As the cultural and political capitals of Greece, these two cities would become crucial to the future of Christianity. Where previously Paul and his associates had stayed at their various mission stations only a matter of days or weeks at the most, now they settled in for a much longer period in Greece. The reason is not hard to figure out: If the Good News was to be carried also to the Gentile world, here was the place to give it the best launching possible. Paul, however, would never change the pattern he had used so successfully in proclaiming the Gospel: First confront Jews with the glad news, then the Gentiles; give the best witness possible, then let the Holy Spirit take care of the rest.

1 The Areopagus at Athens (17:16–34)

While Paul was waiting for Silas and Timothy to join him at Athens, he was far from idle. Obviously he took in the great classical sights at Athens. All of the gleaming marble structures on the Acropolis, including the Parthenon, would have been standing at that time and in much better repair than today. But he had more important work to do. Rather than wait until the rest of his missionary team joined him, Paul started a one-man crusade, teaching in both the synagogue and the agora—the marketplace or civic center at Athens, just northwest of the Acropolis.

Verse 16—He found "the city was full of idols" and it "greatly distressed" him. Conscious of God's commandment against idolatry, any Jew or Jewish Christian (like Paul) would have been rankled by the sight of these many idols. The fact that the cultured Greeks, who gave the world its rules of logic, should have been illogical enough to believe in gods created by humans was too much for Paul, and he cried out against the idolatry to any who would listen.

Verses 18–19—Luke mentions two groups of listeners—Epicureans and Stoics—who debated with Paul and then brought him up to the Areopagus. This is a most accurate historical touch, since the principal philosophical schools in Athens at this time were these two very practical philosophies. Epicureanism, founded by Epicurus of Samos (341–270 B.C.), taught that the chief goal in life was happiness, best achieved by cutting away all annoyances that trouble mankind, especially fear of the gods and the fear of death. The Stoics, founded by Zeno of Citium (approximately 332–262 B.C.), stressed human equality and the need to accept courageously whatever was inevitable in life. Both schools were making a strong impression also in Rome and elsewhere in the Empire.

The Greek name *Areopagus* meant the "rocky crag" or "hill" of Ares, the god of war in Greek mythology. (His name was Mars in Latin, hence the familiar term "Mars' Hill.") Like the *agora*, the Areopagus remains visible to the present day, a huge mass of gray rock looming over Athens just northwest of the Acropolis.

Verses 20–21—These Athenian philosophers, however, were not so set in their ways that they would ignore new teachings. In fact, Luke points out that in the cosmopolitan climate of Athens in that day, new ideas were a big item: "All the Athenians and the foreigners who lived there spent their time doing nothing but talking about and listening to the latest ideas." New was *in*! So Paul had a ready-made audience in Athens.

Verse 22—Paul's address to the Athenians is fascinating, for it shows the best of his sermon technique. Paul opened by complimenting his audience: "Men of Athens! I see that in every way you are very religious." In our secular age today, this may not be thought complimentary, but it was regarded as a compliment in that day. Paul always began his addresses before Greeks and

Romans with respect and graciousness rather than shock or sensationalism.

Verses 23–25—Paul also knew how to use the power of illustration. He reported seeing one of their altars inscribed, "TO AN UNKNOWN GOD," and he brilliantly used this as a device to lock their attention on to his message. To the Athenians, who had hedged their spiritual bets by assigning an altar to placate any unknown deity overlooked in the pantheon of gods and goddesses the Greeks were expected to worship, Paul now revealed the glorious God, the Creator, in the singular—who was far, far greater than the Athenians' deities, since He needed neither temple nor tending.

Verse 26—Paul's comment about God's creative work—"from one man [blood origin] He made every nation of men"—probably found a very responsive chord among his Stoic hearers, who taught something quite similar in their concept of God. Verse 28—His quotations from the Greek writers Epimenides and Aratus demonstrate that Paul of Tarsus was at home in Greek literature.

Paul also delivered a larger concept of God than is often preached or taught. Verse 27—The God Paul announced at Athens is the universal Creator, who is very interested in other nations besides Israel, who is pleased to have mankind grope after Him in various halting ways, and who is an immensely understanding and forgiving God. But with God's ultimate revelation in Christ, enough of the groping: Verses 30–31—"In the past God overlooked such ignorance, but now He commands all people everywhere to repent. For He has set a day when He will judge the world with justice by the man He has appointed. He has given proof of this to all men by raising Him from the dead."

For all their groping, people will never discover the true God; so God has revealed Himself to them through the Gospel of Jesus Christ, and He is causing this Gospel to be proclaimed throughout the world. This Gospel offers salvation to all who receive it, but it warns of condemnation for all who reject it. The transition to Jesus and the heart of the Gospel is natural and logical: Christ is not thrust abruptly into the ears of uncomprehending hearers. No sloganeering for Paul.

At the same time, of course, this man who was never ashamed of the Gospel immediately affirmed one of its great stumbling blocks, the resurrection of the dead—a ridiculous notion for any sophisticated Greek. Verses 32–34—The reaction among his hearers was predictably negative and yet, surprisingly, positive too. While some mocked, others said, "We want to hear you again on this subject." Among those who did were Dionysius, a member of the Areopagus, and a woman named Damaris. These were Paul's first Athenian converts. Whatever became of them is not known, but today's visitor to Athens easily recalls them.

Even if Paul may have thought his mission to Athens less than successful statistically, Mars' Hill and the Acropolis stand today at the intersection of two streets in modern Athens named "Avenue of Dionysius the Areopagite," and "St. Paul's Street." And Paul's address is engraved on a bronze plaque embedded at the base of Mars' Hill today.

2 The Eighteen Months at Corinth (18:1–11)

Paul left Athens for Corinth, 50 miles to the west, the most commercial of the cities of ancient Greece. Corinth was perfectly situated on an isthmus to control all land traffic moving north and south, as well as all sea travel moving east and west. Before the present Corinthian Canal was cut, ships were portaged across the narrows over rolling logs.

Corinth would become central to Paul's mission in Greece, for he stayed there a year and a half. Verses 2–3—To support himself, he returned to tentmaking, and it was in this connection that he fell in with Aquila and Priscilla, a Jewish couple who worked the same trade. They had recently arrived from Rome, because the emperor Claudius had issued an edict in A.D. 49 expelling Jews from that city. Aquila and Priscilla not only converted to Christianity (whether before or after their meeting with Paul is not clear), but they also became close associates of Paul for the rest of his ministry.

Verses 4–8—Again Paul launched his mission by debating in the synagogue each Sabbath day, and soon Silas arrived with Timothy to help him. As elsewhere, some believed, including Crispus, the ruler of the synagogue, whom Paul baptized. But many did not, and once again the missionaries turned to the Gentiles.

A man named Titius Justus offered his home for Christian worship in Corinth, and his home served as Paul's headquarters for a growing mission effort over the next 18 months, which saw an astonishing number of converts. Verses 9–10—Paul himself was firmed up in his efforts here when, as Luke tells it: "One night the Lord spoke to Paul in a vision: 'Do not be afraid; keep on speaking, do not be silent. For I am with you, and no one is going to attack and harm you, because I have many people in this city.'"

Understandably, the Jews of Corinth were nettled at these developments. First, the ruler of their own synagogue converted to Christianity, and then—with all the subtlety of a tidal wave—the Christians started holding services directly *next door* to their synagogue! That is where Justus's house happened to be located (v. 7), near the *agora*. And so, with the increasing number of conversions to what they considered a heretical sect next door to them, the Jews of Corinth apprehended Paul and brought him before the city court.

3 The First "Test Case" for Christianity (18:12–17)

Verse 12—No mere city magistrate awaited them at the tribunal. Sitting on the marble platform in the center of the southern agora at Corinth was no less than the Roman governor of all Greece, L. Junius Gallio, officially titled "Proconsul of Achaea." When Rome took over Greece, it made Corinth (not Athens) its provincial capital, and so the governor's headquarters were in this city.

Verse 13—The prosecution opened its case against Paul with the words, "This man is persuading the people to worship God in ways contrary to the law." Unquestionably, the ominous parallel was not lost on Paul: here, for the second time, a leading Christian was facing a Roman governor who had the power of life and death over him. Would Gallio go Pilate's route, and he, Christ's? Verse 14—Unlike Jesus, however, Paul would have much to say in his own defense. He opened his mouth to speak, but Gallio interrupted him.

Verses 14–15—"If you Jews were making a complaint about some misdemeanor or serious crime," the governor announced, frowning at the prosecution, "it would be reasonable for me to listen to you. But since it involves questions about words and names and your own law—settle the matter yourselves. I will not be a judge of such things." Then he threw the case out of court and cleared the area. Verse 17—Paul's prosecutor, a synagogue official named Sosthenes, now received some buffeting from anti-Semites in the crowd, and although Gallio saw it, he ignored it. So ended what was, in a real sense, the first "test case" of organized Christianity. Had Gallio decided otherwise, Paul's career would have been curtailed or terminated.

Gallio's term as governor in Greece can be dated to A.D. 51–52, due to the exciting discovery of four stone fragments at Delphi, 50 miles northwest of Corinth, on which a communication from the emperor Claudius to the city of Delphi, datable to A.D. 51–52, is inscribed with a reference to "Junius Gallio, my friend, and [pro] consul [of Achaea] …" This inscription has become an anchor for Pauline chronology. Because Roman proconsuls held office for only one year, or, less frequently, for two, this must have been the time of this confrontation in Corinth.

As does history, the stones, then, corroborate Luke also. No archaeological site in the world better reflects Paul's ministry than Corinth. Besides the marble block from the synagogue, excavations along the southern edge of the agora have uncovered the large marble-faced bema or tribunal before which Paul stood. A plaza near the theater at Corinth is paved with limestone blocks, one of which is inscribed, in translated Latin, "Erastus, during his aedileship, laid this pavement at his own expense." The Latin *aedile* means the "manager" of the city. Even the "meat market" Paul refers to in 1 Corinthians 10:25 is mentioned in an inscription, and it, too, seems to have stood near the house church and synagogue along the Lechaion Road.

4 The Return to Antioch (18:18–22)

Verse 18—By now almost three years had passed on the second mission journey, and it was high time to return home. Priscilla and Aquila accompanied Paul on a voyage that began at Cenchrea, Corinth's eastern port on the other side of the isthmus. The fact that Luke mentions Priscilla first in this instance—and again in 18:26 and Romans 16:3—may indicate the prominent role she and other women played in early Christianity.

Also at Cenchrea, either Paul or Aquila "had his hair cut off … because of a vow he had taken." Paul probably is intended, and this was likely a temporary Nazirite vow, referred to in Numbers 6:5. Jews took various vows, often to express thanks for deliverance from danger, and this act of shaving spelled the end of the vow.

Did Paul, as a Christian, *have* to do something like this? Certainly not. But in a letter he would later write to the Corinthians, he explained it well: "Though I am free and belong to no man, I make myself a slave to everyone, to win as many as possible. To the Jews I became like a Jew, to win the Jews. To those under the law I became like one under the law (though I myself am not under the law), so as to win those under the law" (1 Corinthians 9:19–20).

Verse 19—Paul and his Roman friends sailed to Ephesus, where Paul taught briefly in the synagogue. Verses 20–21—He had had his eyes on Ephesus for many months, and the Jews there asked him to stay longer. "Not this time," he replied, in effect. But "I will come back if it is God's will." God certainly must have willed, since this city would be the target of Paul's third mission journey and his three-year ministry there. Then he sailed to Caesarea, greeted the Christians in Jerusalem, and reported to his sponsoring church back home in Antioch.

Conclusion

This was the close of Paul's most spectacular advance for Christ in the Mediterranean world. The seed had been well planted in Europe, and it would sprout and thrive. Luke did not intend to provide a daily diary of everything Paul accomplished, so we must assume that many other smaller churches were planted during this long journey for Jesus. Phoebe suggests a case in point. She emerges out of the blue in Romans 16:1 as a "servant [deaconess] of the church in Cenchrea," but nowhere in the New Testament is there a reference to the founding of the church at Cenchrea or many other churches mentioned in the epistles. Paul and his associates, then, were busier than we ever knew, and God's great blessings on their enterprise mightier than we ever knew. But Paul's most audacious mission was yet to come.

One of the clear lessons to emerge from this segment of Acts is what we might call "consistent Christianity." Believers today often worry about whether their faith will mix properly with politics or society, culture or education. Defensively, they often compartmentalize their beliefs into an "only on Sunday" basis. That, clearly, was *not* Paul's way with the faith! With incredible boldness, he proclaimed Christianity in the very citadel of ancient culture and power, taking on philosophers and answering governors. We could use a touch of that sort of steady, unwavering boldness today!

Concluding Activities

Speak a brief prayer, thanking God for those people who assist the LifeLight participants as they serve the Lord in their own individual ministries. Make any necessary announcements and distribute study leaflet 5.

A Ministry of Miracles (Paul's Third Mission Journey)

Acts 18:23–20:38

Preparing for the Session

Central Focus

Paul's third missionary journey included a three-year ministry in Ephesus, where he established the church in that important center of Asia (today's western Turkey). From there he revisited Macedonia and Greece (Achaia) and made his way back to the Holy Land by way of the coast of Asia.

Objectives

That participants, led by the Holy Spirit, will

1. be more aware of the difference between the Gospel and the beliefs and values frequently found in the world about us;
2. desire to avoid all forms of superstition and occult practices;
3. be willing to teach and guide fellow Christians in a way that will bring their understanding and beliefs more in line with the Gospel;
4. value Christian fellowship.

Note for the small-group leader: Lesson notes and other materials you will need begin on page 67.

For the Lecture Leader

Use a large map of the Mediterranean world at Paul's time to help with your lecture presentation.

Session Plan

Worship

While kneeling was a common prayer posture in the Bible, so was standing with one's arms raised, offering praise to God. The early church developed the custom of standing during prayer to symbolize the resurrection. Tertullian, an early church leader, even insisted that "Fasting and kneeling in worship on the Lord's Day is unlawful." Have the assembly stand with their hands raised for opening prayer. (Use the prayer in the study leaflet or a prayer of your own.) You might add that when we extend our arms outward, offering praise to God, we form a tunnel into which God pours His blessings.

Continue with the hymn. Accompaniments are available in denominational hymnals, such as *Lutheran Worship* (refer to hymnal index). Note: Concordia Publishing House has available *Every Voice a Song*, a 9-CD set of organ accompaniments for 180 hymns and liturgy. All the initial worship hymns in the LifeLight courses are included in this resource. It's especially helpful for mission congregations and small parishes. See the list of study resources on page 6.

Devotion (optional)

A newspaper editor, speaking to a group of high school students, asserted, "We often hear about many different issues—political issues, racial issues, justice issues, educational issues, health issues. In actuality, in this world there is only one issue—the economic issue. Every issue finally boils down to money—who gets it and who doesn't."

You may not agree with that assessment. But it did appear to be the case in Ephesus when Paul ran into powerful opposition to the Gospel. The reason behind that opposition? Money. Paul was opposed by a group of people who made their money by selling silver shrines of Artemis, a goddess whose worship was centered there. They were concerned that the spread of the Gospel would discredit the worship of Artemis and cut into their profits.

The Gospel still faces opposition when it meets head-on the things this world values. Such opposition may not take the form of a riot; it may be much more subtle. Christians may be urged to soften their criticism of sinful lifestyles and practices. They may be advised that they will get further in this world if they accommodate their scruples and consciences to what everybody else is doing. There are even times when Christian moral stands will evoke threats and violence.

In the case of the riot in Ephesus the threatened violence was deflected. But Paul was ready to stand by the Gospel, even when it jeopardized his own personal well-being and safety, as he showed on many other occasions. He was convinced that God would stand by him and sustain him, even if he should be called upon to suffer for the sake of Jesus, who had suffered for him.

May God give us such a courage that is based on confidence in God's mercy and love!

Lecture Presentation

Introduction

Paul and his associates certainly *did* get to the Roman province of Asia and its chief city, Ephesus. In fact, Ephesus holds the record for the longest stay of the apostle during his mission journeys in any one Mediterranean city: three years. There was good reason for this, and Luke describes Paul's activities in Ephesus with much fascinating detail and color. A parade of exotic characters awaits us in Acts 19 and 20: an eloquent but misguided evangelist, seven exorcist brothers, a paranoid silversmith, a fertility goddess, and even a youth named Lucky (who was not!). But all the while, the Christianization of the Mediterranean world continued, as the Holy Spirit inspired both Paul and his hearers.

1 The Ministry of Apollos (18:23–28)

Some early believers in Jesus became missionaries in unusual ways. Verses 24–25—One of these was Apollos of Alexandria in Egypt, who was neither one of the Twelve nor of the Seventy (Luke 10:1). Apollos was a learned and eloquent Jew who had converted to Christianity, but didn't yet have a complete knowledge of the faith. Not daunted, Apollos arrived at Ephesus and started speaking boldly about Jesus in the synagogue there, much as Saul of Tarsus had done years earlier just after his own conversion. Verse 26—Listening to him in the congregation were none other than Paul's tentmaking co-workers, Priscilla and Aquila, who invited Apollos to their home and corrected his immature understanding of Baptism, since he "knew only the baptism of John."

Verses 27–28—A quick learner, Apollos soon became a fully qualified Christian evangelist. Armed with letters of recommendation from the Christians of Ephesus, he now traveled to Corinth and powerfully "watered" what Paul had "planted" there (1 Corinthians 3:6). Because of his specialty in relating Jesus to Hebrew Scripture, Apollos may very well have authored the New Testament Letter to the Hebrews. Apollos, in any case, symbolizes the dozens, perhaps hundreds, of other emissaries for the faith in various parts of the Near East and the Mediterranean.

2 Paul Teaches at Ephesus (19:1–20)

Verse 1—Meanwhile, after resting several months, Paul undertook yet a third mission expedition, once again taking the highway northwestward from Antioch, through the Cilician Gates, and onward to the churches he had founded in Galatia and Phrygia. This was now the third time he had visited Derbe, Lystra, Iconium, and Antioch in the "interior regions" of Asia Minor, which showed their importance to Paul.

On the second mission journey, Paul had veered northwestward to the Dardanelles, but this time he turned toward Ephesus in the southwest, the leading metropolis in the Roman province of Asia. Located three miles from the Aegean, though connected to it by the Cayster River, Ephesus was a rich commercial center like Corinth, yet it also sheltered the wildest collection of pagan priests, magicians, exorcists, cultists, religious prostitutes, and charlatans in the Roman Empire. Since the great marble temple of Artemis was the pride of Ephesus and one of the fabled Seven Wonders of the Ancient World, the city annually played host to hordes of pagan pilgrims from all over the East during the festival of Artemis in March–April. These facts were not lost on Paul of Tarsus, and his mission strategy seems clear: win for Christ in Ephesus and he could win anywhere.

Verses 2–7—Upon arrival in Ephesus, Paul found about a dozen believers who evidently had been converted by Apollos, because they had the same doctrinal deficiency on Baptism, knowing only "John's baptism." Explaining the role of the Holy Spirit and how John the Baptist had pointed to Christ, Paul baptized them "into the name of the Lord Jesus" and laid his hands on them. A small version of Pentecost followed: the Spirit, tongues, and prophecy.

Verses 8–10—For the first three months Paul was permitted to preach his message in the synagogue, until opposition made him withdraw his converts and move over to the "lecture hall of Tyrannus," where he would hold forth on a daily basis for the rest of his ministry at Ephesus. Ancient sources do not identify this Tyrannus, but he seems to have been a Greek teacher or philosopher who owned the hall and rented it to Paul for a nominal fee. Why nominal? Because an alternate Greek text of Acts adds the quite credible phrase that Paul taught in the hall of Tyrannus "from the fifth hour to the tenth," that is, from 11 A.M. till 4 P.M., the hottest part of the day when, presumably, Tyrannus's students had vacated the hall. Such a schedule would permit Paul to earn his living as a tentmaker in the mornings (20:34) and still be able to teach in the afternoons, when his hearers had also abandoned their own labors in the heat of the day.

Verses 11–14—His audience must have been a large ethnic mixture of Jews and Gentiles, Asiatics and Greeks, educated and illiterate, rich and poor, the conventional but also the weird. Ephesus was such a center for ancient magic that books on the occult were often called "Ephesia Grammata" (Ephesian writings) in that day. It was only natural, then, that cousins-by-profession of Simon Magus or Bar-Jesus of Cyprus should be concentrated here. Among such were seven sons of a priest named Sceva, all itinerant Jewish exorcists who were so impressed by Paul's healings in the name of Jesus that they decided to invoke that name too, merely as a magic charm and without any belief in Christ. (This remains the great difference between religion and magic: in the former, personality and faith are involved; in the latter, only formulas and forces.) Gathering around a victim of demon possession in his own house, the seven sons of Sceva began their solemn exorcism with the words, "In the name of Jesus, whom Paul preaches, I command you to come out."

Verses 14–16—"Jesus I know," the evil spirit interrupted, "and I know about Paul, but *who are you?*" Instantly, the demoniac leaped on all seven, tore their clothes off, and gave them a terrible pummeling before they were able to flee the premises, bruised and naked. Paul appears to have cured him in fact, because this incident was all over the streets of Ephesus before the day was out, and a hush of reverence for Paul's God started to blanket the pagan metropolis.

Verses 17–20—Many practitioners of the mystical arts abruptly changed professions, gathering their magic textbooks and paraphernalia and burning them in the agora. Among them were some red-faced Christian converts who had secretly been pursuing a parallel interest in the occult. Before the bonfire had turned to embers, materials worth 50,000 silver drachmas (an enormous sum, since a drachma was a day's wage) had been destroyed.

3 The Theater Riot (19:21–41)

Verses 21–27—Now one of the most dramatic scenes in all of Paul's travels took place at Ephesus. A silversmith named Demetrius was making his fortune by producing statuettes of the goddess Artemis and miniature silver models of her temple in Ephesus—much like the tourist trinkets still available at that Turkish site today. But business had been falling off in a direct proportion to Paul's mission successes. The relationship was not lost on Demetrius.

Calling a meeting of all craftsmen in the Ephesian metalworking guild, Demetrius delivered an emotional harangue, fuming away about how Paul had tainted both Ephesus and most of the province of Asia with the perfectly awful notion that "man-made gods are no gods at all." (A better slogan Paul could not have devised!) "There is danger," Demetrius continued, "not only that our trade will lose its good name, but also that the temple of the great goddess Artemis will be discredited, and the goddess herself, who is worshiped throughout the province of Asia and the world, will be robbed of her divine majesty."

Verses 28–29—Their profits threatened, the angry craftsmen started shouting, "Great is Artemis of the Ephesians!" Pouring into the street, they kindled a demonstration among the people. The rioters rushed over to the city's massive 24,000-seat theater carved into the side of a mountain looming up from Ephesus.

Two of Paul's companions in travel, Macedonians named Gaius and Aristarchus, were discovered by the silversmiths and dragged into the theater also. Verses 30–31—When Paul learned of it, he wanted to go there too, but the Christians of Ephesus wisely prevented that, as did a timely message from some of his friends among the Asiarchs of the city, who warned him not to venture outside. The Asiarchs were Roman officials whose duty it was to advance the emperor's cult and supervise his festivals in the provinces. Probably they were friendly to Paul because he had finally broken Artemis's religious monopoly in Ephesus, something they had been trying to do for years.

Verses 32–34—Over at the theater a full-scale riot was brewing. The Ephesian Jews prompted one of their number, Alexander, to stand up in the orchestra and make it clear to the crowd that Paul did not represent them. Alexander raised his hands for silence. Then someone yelled that Alexander was a Jew, and bedlam broke out. Most of those in the theater started chanting, "Great is Artemis of the Ephesians!" The craftsmen were nearly as suspicious of Jews as they were of Christians, for Jews, too, taught that "man-made gods are no gods at all."

"Great is Artemis of the Ephesians!" The shouts, now as synchronized and rhythmic as a cheering section at an athletic event, went on for no less than two hours. "Great" she was indeed, at least in the number of breasts, eggs, and other fertility symbols that clutter the surviving statues of the Ephesian goddess. Originally a local fertility goddess like the Phoenician Astarte, she was claimed by the Greeks as Artemis and by the Romans as Diana.

Verses 35–41—The highest magistrate available in Ephesus during the riot was the city clerk, who soon arrived and quickly quieted the crowd. "Men of Ephesus," he cried, "doesn't all the world know that the city of Ephesus is the guardian of the temple of the great Artemis and of her image, which fell from heaven? Therefore, since these facts are undeniable, you ought to be quiet and not do anything rash." The rest of his address pointed out the innocence of the defendants, as well as the options of orderly court and even legislative procedure available to the silversmiths. With that he dismissed the crowd. Too tired and too hoarse to challenge him further, the throng finally dispersed.

Today we can sit in the very seats so vacated, for the great theater at Ephesus has finally been fully excavated, a magnificent structure in three vast tiers of semicircular marble seats on which the audience faced westward to view the waterfront. Probably the most beautiful boulevard of antiquity, the Arcadian Way, connected the theater with the port of Ephesus, and its pavement still shows crosses cut into the stones by some early Christians there. No one can sit in any of the 24,000 empty seats today and fail to hear a speaker plainly in the orchestra below—and perhaps even the faint echo of a crowd chanting, "Great is Artemis of the Ephesians!"

4 Paul Returns to Macedonia, Greece, and Troas (20:1–12)

Verses 1–6—Soon after the riot, Paul took his leave of the believers in Ephesus and traveled to Greece via Macedonia. Quite naturally he had to see if conditions had improved in Corinth. Factionalism there, problems with speaking in tongues, scandals, and lawsuits had compelled the apostle to write his famed First and Second Letters to the Corinthians, and so he stayed there for three months during the winter of A.D. 56.

He also had been tending a pet project over the previous months. To symbolize the unity of Jewish and Gentile Christians and to show to the believers in Palestine the concern their Gentile brothers and sisters felt for them, Paul was collecting contributions from the Gentile churches on his itinerary. These gifts were for the Jerusalem Christians, who were in need as a result of famine or persecution or both. Such gifts might also help put to rest any suspicions the Jerusalemites might have had about his ministry.

At Corinth he also wrote his longest and greatest epistle, the powerful Letter to the Romans, in which he discussed Law and Gospel more fully than he had ever done previously. He also told the Christians in Rome of his plans for a future visit to the western Mediterranean world, including Rome and perhaps even Spain.

But now it was time to take his collection to Jerusalem. A sea voyage would have been quickest, but when a plot against him was discovered—possibly involving sabotage of the ship—Paul changed his plans and returned overland instead. No details regarding the plot are cited in Acts, other than its origin among Jewish opponents of his ministry. But the land itinerary gave him the opportunity of revisiting the new churches in Berea, Thessalonica, and Philippi, accompanied by what would become a total of eight co-workers, including Luke, who seems to have rejoined Paul at Philippi and would remain at his side from this point on.

Verses 7–12—They spent a week along the Dardanelles at Troas, and on the night before their departure Paul still had so much to tell the Christians there that he actually talked on until midnight. They were meeting in an upper room, where many burning oil lamps warmed the atmosphere and made at least one member of the congregation very sleepy—a young man named Eutychus. Even though his name meant "Lucky" or "Fortunate" in Greek, Eutychus was anything but. Falling asleep, he dropped out of the third-story window where he had been sitting, onto the ground below. Though the youth was "picked up dead" by the crowd, Paul bent over him and said, "Don't be alarmed. He's alive!" And so he was, for soon he revived. The happy congregation now broke out the food, after which Paul and the flock conversed until daybreak.

5 The Farewell at Miletus (20:13–38)

The missionary band then set sail southward along the Aegean coast, past the three great islands of Lesbos, Kios, and Samos, until they finally docked at Miletus. Verses 16–17—Paul "had decided to sail past Ephesus" because he knew he would lose time there in visiting the faithful when he wanted to hurry on to Jerusalem to arrive there by Pentecost. Any further trouble or riot in Ephesus would only have added to the delay. Miletus was only 30 miles away, so Paul sent word to the elders of the Ephesian church to come meet him at Miletus for a final good-bye. Verses 18–35—Paul now had premonitions that this would be his last journey to that area: "The Holy Spirit warns me that prison and hardships are facing me. ... None of you ... will ever see me again."

His manner, though, was hardly mournful. He rather gave the Ephesian elders a bracing mini course in church administration: "Keep watch over yourselves and all the flock of which the Holy Spirit has made you overseers. Be shepherds of the church of God, which He bought with His own blood." Verses 36–38—After a final prayer together and weeping embraces, they saw Paul off to his ship.

Conclusion

Of all Paul's mission experiences, his third journey seems the most "contemporary" in terms of today's culture. Ephesus, with all its weird cults and parareligious practices, seems very much like modern America—awash in quasi-religious movements that range from the New Age to the Moonies. Gurus in Oregon, cults from California, astrology columns in newspapers, sections for the occult in our bookstores, perversions of the Gospel by televangelists—we have them all. Ephesus lives! But Paul sets Christians an example of how to handle Ephesus: rather than running to escape this swamp of depravity by fleeing the scene, entering a monastery, or cloistering his faith, the apostle met all challenges head on. Christ was strong enough to take on this mess—and win. So was Paul, the man in Christ. Today's Christians also have the credentials, the facts, and the Christ to do the same!

Although he *may* have planned more, Paul would undertake no more independent mission travels, at least none recorded in the New Testament. Jewish opponents and the Roman government would intervene to prevent that. Never mind: the three great journeys proved to be more than enough to have the Good News well planted in Asia Minor, Macedonia, and Greece. Only Italy and Rome remained untouched by Paul's ministry, and yet he would soon visit them too—at state expense.

Immediately ahead, however, no triumphal receptions awaited Paul in Jerusalem, no testimonial banquets or gold watches or plaques denoting a job well done. His "rewards" instead were detention and imprisonment, as both Jesus and the Holy Spirit had predicted.

Concluding Activities

Speak a brief prayer, perhaps asking the Holy Spirit to give us boldness and wisdom to meet successfully the opponents of the Gospel in our own day. Then make any necessary announcements and distribute study leaflet 6.

Defending the Ministry—Part 1 (Arrest in Jerusalem)

Acts 21–23

Preparing for the Session

Central Focus

Despite warnings that he would be arrested there, Paul proceeded to Jerusalem. There, as predicted, Paul was falsely accused, became the focus of a riot, and was arrested. He testified before his countrymen and Roman officials and was transferred to Caesarea for his own protection.

Objectives

That participants, led by the Holy Spirit, will

1. understand more clearly that God was directing the course of Paul's apostolic ministry;
2. feel confident that God is guiding the course of their own lives as they faithfully follow the Lord's Word;
3. courageously witness to others about the Lord's grace, guidance, and blessing in their own lives.

Note for the small-group leaders: Lesson notes and other materials you will need begin on page 70.

For the Lecture Leader

A large map of Jerusalem and the temple area would be helpful for the lecture presentation.

Session Plan

Worship

In the opening worship use the same prayer posture (that is, standing) that the participants used during the week. After singing the hymn, use the following devotion, and adapt the prayer in the study leaflet (perhaps first soliciting prayer requests) or use a prayer of your own.

Hymn accompaniments are available in denominational hymnals, such as *Lutheran Worship* (refer to hymnal index). Note: Concordia Publishing House has available *Every Voice a Song*, a 9-CD set of organ accompaniments for 180 hymns and liturgy. All the initial worship hymns in the LifeLight courses are included in this resource. It's especially helpful for mission congregations and small parishes. See the list of study resources on page 6.

Devotion (optional)

"It isn't fair! I didn't do anything, but still I got in all this trouble."

Have you ever had reason to make that complaint?

As we found in our study this week, Paul might have made that complaint. He was minding his own business, completing the requirements of a vow—which he had agreed to at the urging of others—when suddenly he found himself wrongly accused of an offense that fumed the violent hatred of a mob upon him. If he had not been rescued by the intervention of troops, he might have been killed by the mob right then and there.

Paul had been warned that he was headed for trouble. But he went ahead with his plans to visit Jerusalem, confident that God was working things out in his life. Somehow, some way, God's purposes were being fulfilled; Paul was confident of that and received God's assurance that this was so.

We can be confident, also, that when we follow God's will as revealed in His Word, God is also guiding and directing our lives. We may not see reasons at the time for the things that happen to us—and we may feel that life is being unfair to us—but we can know that God is near and that His purpose is working in us and through the things that are happening to us.

Through these undeserved circumstances, God gave Paul wonderful opportunities to witness about God's grace to him. Paul was able to speak the Gospel to many people, including some who were very influential in this world. This, too, was part of God's guiding plan. The Lord may also be giving us opportunities to bear witness. In this way even undeserved hardships may become opportunities to serve the advance of God's kingdom!

Lecture Presentation

Introduction

After the hard-won triumphs by Paul of Tarsus should have come the rewards. It was not to be. In place of victory there was violence. Instead of adulation there was accusation. Rather than prizes there was prison. Nothing of this was fair by the world's standards. But Paul would have been the last to complain. By faith he knew that something of vastly greater importance was being accomplished by his ministry, and that it would be blessed by God in an extraordinary manner. Paul, however, would not meet his reverses like some lazy Stoic, passively turning the cheek and resigning himself to what seemed inevitable. Instead he would defend his ministry boldly, not only to save it, but—most important—to save it for *the future.*

1 Paul's Journey to Jerusalem (21:8–26)

21:8—Docking at Caesarea, Paul and his associates spent some time at the home of Philip the evangelist, Stephen's colleague as "one of the Seven," that same Philip who had opened a mission thrust into Samaria years earlier and been sent by God to witness to the Ethiopian (6:5; 8:5–40). Two great apostles had been reunited. The church's outreach had come full circle.

Verses 10–13—But the joy was overcast with dark premonitions. A prophet named Agabus had arrived at Caesarea, and he performed a symbolic act on Paul. Taking the apostle's belt, he bound his own hands and feet, warning, "In this way the Jews of Jerusalem will bind the owner of this belt and will hand him over to the Gentiles." Danger lay immediately ahead. The friends clustered about the apostle in Caesarea, including Luke (note the "we" at v. 12), urged him not to go to Jerusalem. But Paul was not to be deterred, and replied: "I am ready not only to be bound, but also to die in Jerusalem for the name of the Lord Jesus."

Verses 17–20—When the missionaries reached Jerusalem, they visited James and the elders of the church, delivering to them the Gentile collection. It was there, rather than in Antioch, that Paul reported on his third expedition, and the leaders of the Jerusalem church were thrilled by his account. They also told Paul of "many thousands" of Jewish Christian converts in Palestine.

Verses 20–26—In that group, however, a problem had developed. Some of its more legalistic members—the Judaizers again!—were still carrying on their campaign against Paul, this time charging that in his mission work the apostle was telling not only Gentiles but also Jews to "turn away from Moses" and refrain from circumcising their children. The charge was false—the church leaders knew that—so they proposed that Paul publicly observe Hebrew law by paying for the temple sacrifices of four Jewish Christians who had taken a Nazirite vow (Numbers 6) and then purify himself with them. What follows should be a dire lesson as to the hazards that occur when purists or narrow-minded legalists try to curtail the freedom of the Gospel.

2 Arrest at the Temple (21:27–22:29)

Verse 27—Although he *certainly* had better things to do in Jerusalem, Paul diplomatically agreed to the elders' request. He went through the week-long ritual at the temple and had nearly finished it when disaster struck. A group of Jewish pilgrims from Asia suddenly recognized Paul in the temple precincts and grabbed him.

Verses 28–29—"Men of Israel, help us!" they shouted, and then identified Paul as a teacher who attacked the Jews, the Law, and the temple everywhere he could. "And besides," they added ominously, "he has brought Greeks [i.e., Gentiles] into the temple area and defiled this holy place." This last charge, though only based on speculation, was lethal. Marking off an inner enclosure in the temple were 13 stone slabs that bore the following inscription in Hebrew and Greek: "Let no Gentile enter within the balustrade (railing) and enclosure surrounding the sanctuary. Whoever is caught will be personally responsible for his consequent death." Previously, Paul's accusers had seen him in Jerusalem with an Ephesian Gentile named Trophimus. He had met Paul at Troas (20:4–5) and accompanied him to Jerusalem, probably to represent the Aegean churches in presenting the collection they had raised. Yet Trophimus had *not* accompanied Paul inside the temple as they had supposed. But try to argue with a mob!

Verses 30–36—Paul, then, was one "Roman" Jew from Tarsus whom the enraged crowd that had gathered would dispose of in short order. Paul was dragged out of the temple and was well on his way to getting stoned to death while he doubtless protested that it was all a dreadful mistake.

Fortunately for Paul, the Roman cohort of Jerusalem was stationed in the Tower Antonia, which overlooked the entire temple precinct from its northwestern corner. The uproar brought the Roman commander [tribune] and his troops running out of the Antonia and over to Paul, whom they arrested and chained. Because the throng now pressed in on every side, yelling, *"Away with him!"* Paul actually had to be carried up the steps in front of the fortress.

Verses 37–40—Just before they moved inside the gate, Paul spoke to the commander in Greek. This surprised the commander, since he had assumed Paul was a trouble-making pseudoprophet from Egypt who had previously led 4,000 men out of the desert to attack Jerusalem. Paul quickly set him straight and then begged permission to address the crowd. Permission was granted.

22:1–21—Using the staircase at the Antonia as his pulpit, Paul delivered his message with passionate honesty, beginning with his background at Tarsus and his education under Gamaliel. He continued by detailing his conversion experience on the Damascus road, and next reported a vision while praying at the Jerusalem temple, in which Jesus had warned him to flee the city and testify instead to the Gentiles.

Verses 22–25—The last was too much for the crowd. They stopped listening and started yelling, *"Rid the earth of him! He's not fit to live!"* Some were throwing handfuls of dust into the air, while others waved their cloaks in what was now an out-and-out riot. The commander immediately ordered Paul inside the Antonia and had him stripped for scourging. With so much shouting by the crowd, the man must have been guilty of something, and a little lashing would wring a confession out of him. Coolly, Paul waited until they had tied him up with thongs before he asked a question with all the subtlety of a Roman battering-ram: "Is it legal for you to flog a Roman citizen who hasn't even been found guilty?"

Verses 26–29—The centurion in charge immediately informed the commander. Astonished and embarrassed, he confirmed the claim of citizenship with Paul before he stated, "I had to pay a big price for my citizenship." His Greek name, Claudius Lysias, showed that purchase had been necessary. "But I was *born* a citizen," Paul could reply proudly. Instantly, he was untied.

3 Paul Addresses the Council (22:30–23:11)

Verse 30—Lysias still had to have an explanation for the riot, so he convened a meeting of the Jewish Sanhedrin the next morning and brought Paul before it, not to try him, but to discover the reason for the furor. 23:1—The hearing got off to a very bad start. Paul began, "My brothers, I have fulfilled my duty to God in all good conscience to this day."

Verse 2—"Strike him on the mouth!" Ananias the high priest ordered someone from the marble benches.

Verse 3—"God will strike *you*, you whitewashed wall!" cried Paul, using the same metaphor for hypocrites that Jesus had used. "You sit there to judge me according to the law, yet you yourself violate the law by commanding that I be struck!" (God's Law required fair trials, Leviticus 19:15.)

Verse 4—Some bystanders now identified Paul's antagonist. "You dare to insult God's *high priest?*" they asked.

Verse 5—Lowering his voice, Paul replied, "Brothers, I did not realize that he was the high priest; for it is written: 'Do not speak evil about the ruler of your people'" (Exodus 22:28). The high priest at the time was Ananias Ben-Nebedaeus, and his unwarranted, arbitrary conduct here correlates well with the cruel streak in his character known from purely Jewish sources. Ananias would later be hunted down and killed by Jewish rebels when they found him hiding in an aqueduct at the start of their war with Rome in A.D. 66.

Verses 6–8—As with other speeches in Acts, Luke has not necessarily provided a complete transcript, and Paul very likely went on with a lengthy defense that was probably terminated by dangerous murmuring or shouting in the Sanhedrin. For now he rather cleverly extricated himself by crying, "My brothers, I am a Pharisee, the son of a Pharisee. I stand on trial because of my hope in the resurrection of the dead."

This statement immediately set the chamber to quarreling, because the majority in the Sanhedrin consisted of Sadducees, who rejected any resurrection, or angel or spirit, whereas the Pharisees upheld them all, as Luke carefully explained. The Pharisees would now serve as at least temporary allies of Paul while the two parties squared off against each other in theological combat.

Verses 9–11—Soon the debate descended to the physical level, and the commander ordered Paul removed for safety. This episode is refreshing, because it shows Paul a very human sort, who was not above using his head to get himself out of a scrape. A larger-than-life saint of God might well have taken a passive, resigned stance before the Sanhedrin. Not Paul. He knew his life's work was not over. That night, he also experienced another reassuring vision of Jesus, who said, "Take courage! As you have testified about Me in Jerusalem, so you must also testify in Rome."

4 The Plot to Kill Paul (23:12–24)

Verses 12–20—During the next day or two at the Antonia fortress, things went well for Paul, who was more under detention than imprisonment. But then his young nephew—his sister's son—visited him. (We do not know their names, nor how many other members there were in Paul's family.) The lad had some alarming news, and Paul thought only a moment before instructing him to carry the information to Lysias. It was nothing less than a plot on Paul's life. The commander would be asked to send Paul back to the Sanhedrin for further questioning. Verse 21—"Don't give in to them," the youth begged Lysias, "because more than forty of them are waiting in ambush for him. They have taken an oath not to eat or drink until they have killed him." Probably they were members of the Zealot or terrorist faction, a Jewish party largely responsible for inciting the revolt against Rome in A.D. 66.

Verses 22–24—The commander's brow wrinkled as he replied to Paul's nephew, "Don't tell anyone that you have reported this to me." Summoning two centurions, the commander ordered them to prepare a guard for about 9 P.M. to conduct Paul safely to Felix, the provincial governor in Caesarea. (Since people went to bed shortly after sundown, 9 p.m. would be more like our midnight in terms of a good time for escapes in the night.) Two hundred soldiers would be needed, again as many spearmen, as well as 70 cavalry. The size of such a guard is astonishing, although if Paul had been discovered within the city and a riot had broken out, all 470 men would have been needed to protect their prisoner—and themselves.

5 Paul Sent to Caesarea (23:25–35)

Verses 31–32—Everything worked as planned. Paul was given a mount to ride, and they reached safety in the Plain of Sharon at Antipatris, a military post between Judea and Samaria about 35 miles northwest of Jerusalem. Only the 70-member cavalry would continue with Paul on to Caesarea. After they had all spent the night in the Roman garrison at Antipatris, the rest of the 400-man guard returned to their barracks in Jerusalem.

Verse 33—Upon arrival at Caesarea, the cavalry brought Paul before Felix and handed the governor a letter from Lysias, detailing the circumstances of Paul's arrest. The letter went on, accurately enough: (vv. 29–30) "I found that the accusation had to do with questions about their law, but there was no charge against him that deserved death or imprisonment. When I was informed of a plot to be carried out against the man, I sent him to you at once. I also ordered his accusers to present to you their case against him."

Verse 34—After reading the letter, Felix asked Paul which of the Roman provinces was his home. The reason for this was to authenticate Paul's claim of citizenship. Lysias had mentioned that citizenship in his letter, and the governor wanted to know where Paul was enrolled. A letter of inquiry to the capital of the province in question would then establish the fact of citizenship—or lack of same, in which case stiff punishment would be in store.

Verse 35—Paul responded, of course, that he was from Tarsus in Cilicia, and most probably added details about the circumstances of how his father or ancestors had gained Roman citizenship. Satisfied for the moment, Felix replied, "I will hear your case when your accusers get here."

During the five days that intervened between Paul's

arrival in Caesarea and that of his accusers, the apostle was kept under guard in Herod's palace. This was the citadel of power in Roman Palestine, seat of the provincial governors. Here is where Pontius Pilate had lived most of the year, and where King Herod Agrippa I had spent his last days following his fatal appearance (12:19b–23). And, although he could not know it at the time, here is also where Paul would remain for two long years, making celebrated appearances before two Roman governors—Felix and Festus—as well as Agrippa's son and daughter, Agrippa II and Bernice.

Conclusion

One may speculate endlessly on other scenarios that could have happened in place of the events leading to Paul's arrest in Jerusalem. We so very much wish that the apostle who had championed the freedom of the Gospel might have had a fourth and fifth mission journey—or more.

A higher plan was at work here, not to be deterred by any decisions at the human level. "In all things" God was indeed working "for the good of those who love Him," as Paul had written the Romans (8:28). His experience at Jerusalem was a case in point. Our experiences are another. No matter what the circumstances, the choice, or the situation may be, the same God arranges everything for the ultimate good of those who believe and trust in Him today—as did the now-imprisoned Paul of Tarsus.

Concluding Activities

Speak a brief prayer, perhaps that you might be bold and courageous in making your own testimony concerning Jesus. Then make any necessary announcements and distribute study leaflet 7.

Defending the Ministry—Part 2 (Imprisonment in Caesarea)

Acts 24–26

Preparing for the Session

Central Focus

Paul is tried before two Roman governors, Felix and Festus, and has a hearing before a king, Agrippa II. Paul appeals to Caesar's judgment of his case and is to be transferred to Rome. At his trials and hearing, Paul witnesses to his faith in Jesus as the Savior and even urges his judges to join him in this faith!

Objectives

That participants, led by the Holy Spirit, will

1. be aware of how Paul used every opportunity to proclaim the Gospel to others;
2. desire to share the Gospel with others at every available opportunity;
3. be more skillful in recognizing and more ready to seize opportunities to speak the Gospel.

Note for the small-group leaders: Lesson notes and other materials you will need begin on page 73.

Session Plan

Worship

In leading the opening devotion, review the comments in the study guide suggesting that there are times when God does not hear prayers or answer them. He tells us that in the Scripture. The reasons why are called "short circuits" in *A Prayer Primer* by Erwin J. Kolb (Concordia Publishing House, 1986). In addition to those mentioned in the study leaflet, other short-circuits to prayer are these: Our iniquities separate us from God (Isaiah 59:1–2); we pray doubting that God will hear and answer (James 1:5–8); we ask wrongly (James 4:3). The writer of Proverbs says, "If anyone turns a deaf ear to the law, even his prayers are detestable" (Proverbs 28:9). Read the Bible passage and prayer in the study leaflet as participants sit with closed fists. You may want to follow the printed prayer with a prayer of your own, but this time with the group sitting relaxed and hands folded. When you introduce the hymn you may point out that even as Jesus once came "in blessing, All our sins redressing," so now we ask Him to "Let us here confess You Till in heav'n we bless You." Hymn accompaniments are available in denominational hymnals, such as *Lutheran Worship* (refer to hymnal index). Note: Concordia Publishing House has available *Every Voice a Song,* a 9-CD set of organ accompaniments for 180 hymns and liturgy. All the initial worship hymns in the LifeLight courses are included in this resource. It's especially helpful for mission congregations and small parishes. See the list of study resources on page 6.

Devotion (optional)

"There we were, to be seated side by side for the next 13 hours. We had never laid eyes on one another before, and likely will not see one another again, but during that long flight we got to know one another well. Of course I told her how important Jesus Christ is to me how my hopes are based in Him, how His forgiveness and love are the foundation of my every day, how He strengthens me for the tasks and challenges facing me, how He guides me through His Word."

Actually, we all have many opportunities to tell others about what Jesus means to us. Those opportunities may be found wherever we interrelate with other people. They may occur over the backyard fence, at a party, even in an elevator.

How about while testifying in court—at your own trial? In our lesson this week we heard that Paul shared his faith in Jesus while testifying at his own trials, urging even his judges to adopt his faith! Talk about making the most of every opportunity!

But that is what we want to do—make the most of every opportunity we have to speak to others about Jesus. That may not come for you while you are on trial—I hope not. But it may come while seated next to a stranger on an airplane or visiting a neighbor in the hospital or on a coffee break at work. Be alert for these opportunities. And when they come, use them to say what you think about Jesus.

Lecture Presentation

Introduction

Once again, the Roman administration in the Mediterranean world was invoked to settle a Jewish-Christian dispute. Since the Romans knew very little about either Judaism or Christianity, theirs was surely the wrong court for such matters. Small wonder that their decisions were delayed, inappropriate, unjust, and finally appealed. Yet somehow, a miscarriage of justice in Judea still resulted in what Paul—and God—had been planning for a long time in any case: his long-awaited mission trip to Rome. With developments like that, it's a small wonder that he was confident of a higher power arranging his destiny. The apostle's mission to the Gentile world was far from over.

1 The Hearing before Felix (24)

Like Gallio (Paul's judge in Corinth), Felix (his judge in Caesarea) is very well known in Roman sources. His rise to power as procurator of Judea—for so the governors were now termed—was from the very pits of Roman society. Felix and his brother Pallas had been slaves at Rome who had somehow won their freedom and were later both appointed to high posts by the emperor Claudius. Previously, Pallas had averted disaster for the emperor Tiberius by alerting him to a conspiracy against him. Serving subsequently as Claudius's finance minister, Pallas became one of the richest and most powerful men in all the empire, and it was doubtless due to his influence that his brother Felix was appointed as governor of Judea in A.D. 52.

For his part, Felix had been marrying repeatedly, but well. In all, he wed three women of royalty: one wife is unknown, another was the granddaughter of Antony and Cleopatra, and his current spouse was a beautiful Jewess named Drusilla, a daughter of King Herod Agrippa I. With his powerful connections in Rome, however, Felix felt he could conduct a government of extortion, cruelty, and oppression in Palestine and get away with it, as even the Roman historian Tacitus admits in pointing to Felix as a prime cause of the great Jewish rebellion against Rome in A.D. 66.

Verse 1—Such was the man who sat on his tribunal before Paul and his accusers, who had now arrived from Jerusalem, five days after Paul. They included the high priest himself, Ananias, and some of the members of the Sanhedrin. Verses 2–4—When Felix called for the accusation, a lawyer-spokesman for the prosecution, one Tertullus, arose and flattered Felix with a flowery, syrupy introduction that was laughably false, though true to Roman court procedure. Then Tertullus lodged his formal indictment of Paul: Verses 5–8—"We have found this man to be a troublemaker, stirring up riots among the Jews all over the world. He is a ringleader of the Nazarene sect and even tried to desecrate the temple; so we seized him. By examining him yourself you will be able to learn the truth about all these charges we are bringing against him."

Verse 9—The Sanhedrists seconded these charges against Paul, supplying whatever evidence they could.

Verse 10—Next, Felix called for the defense. With a far less flattering and more honest introduction, Paul took on all three charges and disposed of them as follows: Verse 12—(1) A pestilent agitator? In Jerusalem, "my accusers did not find me arguing with anyone at the temple, or stirring up a crowd in the synagogues or anywhere else in the city."

Verses 14–15—(2) A ringleader of the Nazarenes? In effect, yes, but so what? Paul admitted to being "a follower of the Way, which they call a sect." Then he continued, "I believe everything that agrees with the Law and that is written in the Prophets, and I have the same hope in God as these men, that there will be a resurrection of both the righteous and the wicked." Thus Paul's thesis here and everywhere: Christianity was the fulfillment of Judaism.

Verses 17–19—(3) Profaner of the temple? This, of course, would have been the easiest charge to disprove, and doubtless Paul had, or would soon get, a deposition from Trophimus (a Gentile who had accompanied Paul from Ephesus) and other witnesses that neither Trophimus nor any other Gentile with Paul had set foot in the sacred precincts. Paul affirmed that he was merely on a charitable mission to Jerusalem and was observing the temple rites when he was attacked by Jewish pilgrims from Asia who "ought to be here before you and bring charges if they have anything against me."

Paul, who knew his Roman law, was absolutely correct on the last point.

Verse 22—Having heard the evidence, Felix pondered the case. Since he "was well acquainted with the Way," as Luke states, he probably realized that the religious dimension of the quarrel was beyond his jurisdiction. Yet, if he simply released Paul, he would further antagonize the Jewish authorities, who likely were building a case against Felix for maladministration. On the other hand, he could not justifiably sentence Paul for any criminal act. Nor could he abandon him to the Sanhedrin, because he was a Roman citizen.

And so—no decision. Felix merely stalled, telling the prosecution that he would decide the case in the future. Meanwhile, he left Paul under loose confinement with some liberties, including unrestricted access to friends. Verse 24–25—But there was something about the apostle that intrigued the governor, and he sent for him repeatedly in months to come. Once, he had Paul speak in the presence of his wife Drusilla too. Knowing Felix's true character, his response is almost humorous: When Paul held forth on "righteousness, self-control and the judgment to come, Felix was afraid and said, 'That's enough for now! You may leave.'" Verse 26—If truth were told, Felix wanted nothing more than a big bribe to release his prisoner, which was quite in character for that governor.

Verse 27—For the next two years Paul was in confinement at Caesarea due to this impasse. Felix kept him incarcerated because he "wanted to grant a favor to the Jews." But the time was not lost. Paul was busy with his letters to the churches. Friends like Philip the evangelist, who was also in Caesarea, would surely have visited him. It was also during these months that Luke most likely visited Jerusalem to learn from the elders there all the many facts about Jesus that the gifted Greek would later work into the Gospel bearing his name. He must also have had special interviews with Mary, the mother of Jesus, who was presumably staying with John at Jerusalem. This would explain Luke's crucial portrayal of the Christmas story, details that only Mary would have known.

2 The Hearing before Festus (25:1–12)

About A.D. 58, Felix was recalled by the emperor Nero, and a delegation of Jews lost no time in sailing to Rome to charge Felix for maladministration. Felix's brother Pallas, however, had enough influence with Nero, even in retirement, to have the charges quashed. After this, Felix and his wife drop out of history.

Verses1–2—The new governor sent to Palestine was Porcius Festus, certainly an improvement on Felix. Quite diplomatically, Festus spent his first days at the religious, not political, capital of Judea—Jerusalem. Verses 2–3—The priests lost no time in bringing Paul's case to the attention of Festus, appealing that he return Paul to detention in Jerusalem rather than Caesarea. In fact, it was another plot on Paul's life: They were planning an ambush to murder him en route, since Festus would not think to guard Paul as well as had Felix. The plotters were likely the same crew that had sworn neither to eat or drink until they had killed Paul—a group that must have been very hungry by this time!

Verses 4–5—Instead, Festus invited Paul's detractors to accompany him to Caesarea and renew their charges there. By later standards, this would probably be deemed double jeopardy in Paul's case, and yet his status was extremely uncertain, due to Felix's mishandling of the case. To put it plainly, Paul was in legal limbo.

Verses 6–8—The Jewish leaders in Jerusalem accepted Festus's suggestion, and Paul soon had a second formal hearing. It was much like the first, except that the prosecution seemed to have even less evidence after the two-year lapse. Besides, the high priest Ananias was deposed about this time, so the charges against Paul were flimsy at best. Had Festus been firmly in office for some months, he doubtless would have released Paul. But he was a newcomer, quite anxious to please his new subjects and still treat Paul fairly. Verse 9—He thought he had the perfect solution in a rather naive suggestion for Paul: "Are you willing to go up to Jerusalem and stand trial before me there on these charges?"

"Twenty-four months in confinement for this?" Paul must have thought, struggling to keep his temper under control. Any hearing back in Jerusalem would have been in a climate hopelessly prejudged against him and presided over by an inexperienced governor trying to win favor with his new subjects. Paul would simply have lost his case, his freedom, and probably his life.

Verses 10–11—Instead, he made a statement that would change his life irrevocably, and he uttered it with passion: "I am now standing before Caesar's court, where I ought to be tried. I have not done any wrong to the Jews, as you yourself know very well. If, however, I am guilty of doing anything deserving death, I do not refuse to die. But if the charges brought against me by these Jews are not true, no one has the right to hand me over to them. I appeal to Caesar!" It was his right as a Roman citizen.

Verse 12—Festus immediately turned to confer with his advisers. After some shoulder-shrugging and head nodding from them, Festus faced the prisoner with his decision: "You have appealed to Caesar. To Caesar you will go!" Then he cleared the court.

3 The Hearing before Agrippa (25:13–26:24)

In the next days Festus had more of a problem than Paul, who suddenly found his long-planned trip to Rome underwritten by the state. The Caesar (emperor) at this time was Nero. Although he already had several crimes to his credit, he was not yet the shocking ruler that history would come to know so well. Nero was still a youth (in his early 20s) at this time, and it was his tutor, Seneca, who virtually ran the government for him during those first five years. Seneca did so noble a job that the later emperor Trajan regarded that five-year period as the best government Rome ever had. Paul's appeal, then, was an extremely shrewd way to bypass a miscarriage of justice at Caesarea.

Festus, however, dared not send Paul on to Rome without definite charges against him, and he had been unable to determine such charges. Verses 13–21—He raised this problem before the son and daughter of the dead King Agrippa—Herod Agrippa II and his sister Bernice, who had just arrived in Caesarea to pay a visit of welcome to the new governor. Agrippa II was only 17 when his father died and was thought too young to succeed him. In the meantime, he had become ruler over lands northeast of Palestine. His attractive sister Bernice was one of the extraordinary Herodian princesses.

Married three times, she was undoubtedly carrying on an incestuous relationship with her brother Agrippa II, and she would eventually become mistress of no less than Titus, the future Roman emperor.

Verse 23—Interested in hearing Paul speak, this unlikely couple entered the audience hall at their father's onetime palace with great pomp and ceremony for the scheduled interview. The Roman officers' corps and civic leaders were also present in the chamber. Verses 24–25—Porcius Festus now announced the legal history of Paul's case, including his appeal. Verse 26—Then he added, "But I have nothing definite to write to His Majesty [Nero] about him. Therefore I have brought him … before you, King Agrippa, so that as a result of this investigation I may have something to write."

26:2–21—Paul offered one of his most impassioned defenses, reporting again his conversion and subsequent ministry. Again he rooted all his claims about Christ in Old Testament Scripture, pointing out how perfectly Jesus fulfilled the parameters of messianic prophecy. Again he announced the ultimate proof for that messiahship in Jesus' resurrection from the dead. That core of Christianity was also the heart of Paul's preaching, whether in the marketplace, at court, or in a royal audience hall.

Verses 22–23—His defense culminated in the words: "But I have had God's help to this very day, and so I stand here and testify to small and great alike. I am saying nothing beyond what the prophets and Moses said would happen—that the Christ would suffer and, as the first to rise from the dead, would proclaim light to His own people and to the Gentiles."

Verse 24—"You are out of your mind, Paul!" Festus interrupted. "Your great learning is driving you insane!"

4 Agrippa's Verdict (26:25–32)

Verses 25–26—Continuing his focus on Agrippa, Paul pointed out that the king could corroborate some of his claims, because matters involving Jesus were "not done in a corner." Verse 27—Finally, Paul put it to him point-blank: "King Agrippa, do you believe the prophets? I know you do."

Verse 28—In response, Agrippa asked, "Do you think that in such a short time you can persuade me to be a Christian?"

Verse 29—"Short time or long," Paul replied, "I pray God that not only you but all who are listening to me today may become what I am, except for these chains."

Verse 30—With this, Agrippa II stood up and ended the hearing. Verse 31—As he was retiring with Festus and Bernice, they voiced a common opinion: "This man is not doing anything that deserves death or imprisonment." Verse 32—Agrippa remarked that Paul "could have been set free if he had not appealed to Caesar." In other words, once Paul had appealed to the emperor, he became inextricably enmeshed in the Roman legal system and had to see his case through at Rome. But the apostle was not in error at having made the original appeal: at the time, it most likely saved his life.

More important is the fact that somehow Luke learned of Agrippa's crucial remarks, else he could not have recorded them in Acts. Doubtless he and Paul would make excellent use of this statement as something of a deposition in the future hearing before Nero. Here was a Jewish king—one who would know all the fine points of Jewish law that Paul was supposed to have violated—who declared that Paul could have been set free.

Agrippa II, then, was a much fairer individual than his colorful but violent father, Agrippa I, who enjoyed making "the grand gesture," even if it meant cutting off the head of James the apostle or putting Peter in prison (12:1–5). His son, on the other hand, was cut from different stuff. Seven or eight years later, he would stand in a rioting Jerusalem and counsel moderation as he *tried* to keep his countrymen from rebelling against Rome. He would fail.

Paul, however, would succeed in carrying his case—and above all, his Gospel—to Rome.

Conclusion

With impassioned honesty, Paul had indeed defended his ministry both in Jerusalem and in Caesarea. No, Agrippa was not really on the point of converting to Christianity, but he must have felt the profound genuineness in Paul's presentation. The man truly believed what he was saying. This was why Paul never tired of reporting his conversion experience on the road to Damascus—three times in the Book of Acts. Jesus had appeared to him on the Damascus road, Paul knew, and this is what had transformed a Jewish fanatic into a Christian missionary. And because Christ had also commissioned him to proclaim the Good News, he had become an apostle too, even without benefit of membership among the original 12 disciples. Now he could endure everything from catcalls to chains, trials, or torture—it made no difference. Nothing could or would separate him from the love of God in Christ Jesus, as he wrote so eloquently to the Romans (8:39)—not even shipwreck, and that was next on the schedule.

Here, then, is the secret of how Christians today can be happy under any circumstances, whether they are faced with good fortune or disaster, freedom or chains. Paul's time in prison was only the living out of his great claim in Romans 8:38–39: "For I am convinced that neither death nor life, neither angels nor demons, neither the present nor the future, nor any powers, neither height nor depth, nor anything else in all creation, will be able to separate us from the love of God that is in Christ Jesus our Lord."

A conviction like that should be a motto for us all, serving very well in the present tense in which Paul wrote it.

Concluding Activities

Speak a brief prayer, perhaps for the courage to speak up for the Gospel about Jesus on any occasion. Then make any necessary announcements and distribute study leaflet 8.

The Castastrophic Voyage to Rome

Acts 27

Preparing for the Session

Central Focus

The sea voyage that took Paul to Rome began late in the sailing season, was delayed by contrary winds, and included a terrifying interruption when the ship was wrecked after a violent storm. But God rescued all on the ship for the sake of Paul, His apostle.

Objectives

That participants, led by the Holy Spirit, will

1. understand how the Lord preserved the lives of Paul and his traveling companions for the sake of Paul's Gospel ministry, which was to be continued in Rome;
2. grow more confident of the Lord's direction and protection as they carry out their own service to the Lord;
3. show greater courage in times of crisis on account of this confidence resulting from faith;
4. thank and praise God for His protection and guidance.

Note for the small-group leaders: Lesson notes and other materials you will need begin on page 76.

For the Lecture Leader

If at all possible, use a map to point out locations as you make your lecture presentation.

Session Plan

Worship

As you conduct the opening worship, it may seem awkward to use this week's prayer posture of kneeling in a large assembly, but encourage it anyway and set the example. Jesus was uncomfortable too when He knelt in Gethsemane to pray (Luke 22:41). Some of the participants will have knelt for prayer all week at home but some may never have knelt in prayer in their adult lives. Acknowledge that some with knee problems may want to kneel on one knee and that those who cannot get down may sit with their hands folded and heads bowed, leaning forward in their seats. If you can, share some of your own experiences with kneeling for prayer, either in your private devotions, a prayer meeting, or in a group assembly. Focus on how you felt during those times. If there is time, ask some of the class members to share how they felt when they tried this prayer posture at home.

In introducing the hymn you may want to remind the worshipers of the great privilege we have of speaking directly to the one true God—Father, Son, and Holy Spirit. Hymn accompaniments are available in denominational hymnals, such as *Lutheran Worship* (refer to hymnal index). Note: Concordia Publishing House has available *Every Voice a Song*, a 9-CD set of organ accompaniments for 180 hymns and liturgy. All the initial worship hymns in the LifeLight courses are included in this resource. It's especially helpful for mission congregations and small parishes. See the list of study resources on page 6.

Devotion (optional)

Courage may come from one of two sources—from confidence in one's own powers or from confidence that one stands under the protection of someone else's superior powers.

In our study this week we found the apostle Paul, by his own courage, inspiring heart and hope in the crew and passengers of a ship about to be wrecked at sea in a furious storm. Where did Paul find this courage that held his terrified shipmates together and directed them to taking measures that would result in the survival of every person while the ship itself was battered to pieces by pounding waves? It was not the force of Paul's own unconquerable personality that accomplished this feat but the conviction that he and his shipmates were under the protection of God, the Lord of wind and waves. Paul's trust in God's promise was the source of his courage.

And that same source may also give us courage, even in the face of disaster. We also may take courage in the conviction that God claims us as His own and will not desert us, that His strength will see us through. Paul himself expressed this foundation for our courage when he wrote in his Letter to the Romans: "He who did not spare His own Son, but gave Him up for us all—how will He not also, along with Him, graciously give us all things? ... I am convinced that neither death nor life, neither angels nor demons, neither the present nor the future, nor any powers, neither height nor depth, nor anything else in all creation, will be able to separate us from the love of God that is in Christ Jesus our Lord" (Romans 8:32–39).

Lecture Presentation

Introduction

Chapter 27 of Acts is one of the finest—if not *the* finest—description of ancient nautical, maritime, and meteorological matters in any sources from the first century—sacred or secular. The entire episode breathes realism and authenticity. Beyond all debate, the author *must* have been an eyewitness—Luke who accompanied Paul on the voyage to Rome. Aside from the literary distinction, however, this segment in Acts also shows Paul's faith put to a very practical test: Would it serve him in a life-threatening storm? When nature was on a rampage, no army or judge could intervene to save his life, no appeal to the emperor would have any effect. This time, the storm was worse than anything possible on the Sea of Galilee, and Jesus was not in the same boat to still the tempest. Or was He?

1 Sailing to Crete (27:1–13)

A ship bound for the Aegean had put in at the port of Caesarea and, since it was not a military vessel, Aristarchus of Thessalonica and faithful Luke were allowed to sail along as Paul's traveling companions. Apparently, Aristarchus also had been at Paul's side ever since his ministry in Macedonia and had barely escaped with his life during the silversmiths' riot at Ephesus during the third mission journey (19:29).

Verses 1–3—Paul had been placed in the custody of a centurion named Julius, about whom we know very little. But apparently he and his detail of guards had come to know the apostle well enough during his months in prison at Caesarea to treat him kindly and permit him some liberties. When the ship sailed off on an overnight run 70 miles northward to Sidon, Julius allowed Paul to go ashore and visit the Christians in that Phoenician port.

Verses 4–5—From Sidon they had planned a direct northwesterly voyage toward the Aegean, but stiff winds from that heading made them sail under the leeward side of Cyprus, using the long northeastern peninsula of that island as a shield as they made their way northeastward around that finger of land until they could resume a westward journey under the protection of Asia Minor. They finally docked at the port of Myra in southwestern Asia Minor. Verse 6—There Julius found a huge Alexandrian grain ship bound for Italy and transferred his party aboard it.

On the largest ships afloat on the Mediterranean, merchant marines worked the famed Italy-Egypt-Italy grain shuttle, which sailed during the summer months in a counterclockwise rotation. Leaving the Bay of Naples and heading southeastward to Sicily with pottery, metalware, and passengers, these ships caught the northwesterly winds beyond the straits and ran before them directly to Alexandria in a brisk voyage of two weeks or less. Unloading cargo in Egypt, they took on tons of wheat there and new passengers, returning to Italy against the winds via a roundabout route that saw them sail on a zigzag course past Palestine, Asia Minor, and Greece.

Verse 7—It was on this leg of the shuttle that Paul and 275 other passengers set sail from Myra. A powerful but contrary wind was no help at all. They inched along the south coast of Asia Minor and past Rhodes into the rougher waters of the Aegean. Now no longer shielded by land, they decided to sail under the protection of Crete for shelter from the northwesterlies. Verse 8—Rounding the eastern cape of that island, they coasted along with difficulty until dropping anchor at a small bay called Fair Havens in the south central coast of Crete.

Verse 9—Since "by now it was after the Fast" (i.e., the Day of Atonement in early October), they were now in the danger interim on the Mediterranean beyond what the Romans called "safe sailing" and near the period of winter's "closed sea," from November 10 through March 10.

Verse 10—Thus they had gone far enough for that sailing season, Paul concluded, because so much time had been lost to contrary winds. "Men," he told the captain and staff, "I can see that our continuing voyage is going to be disastrous and bring great loss to ship and cargo, and to our own lives also." Paul knew the Mediterranean and its habits from his boyhood on the sea near Tarsus, as well as from personal experience: "Three times I was shipwrecked," he had written earlier, "I spent a night and a day in the open sea" (2 Corinthians 11:25).

Verses 11–12—The owner of the ship happened to be a passenger also, and he discussed Paul's opinion with the captain and with Julius, the centurion. They chose to gamble on a last run along the coast to a better wintering port on Crete named Phoenix, 40 miles farther west, since Fair Havens was little more than an anchorage. Why spend the winter in an only partially enclosed harbor, open to the east and southeast where winter winds could blow directly into the bay? Phoenix was much better protected from stormy easterlies and was a town with far more conveniences.

Verse 13—A gentle, reliable south wind started blowing, so they weighed anchor and sailed westward with it, close inshore and very carefully. One can almost see Julius jovially tweaking Paul's gray beard on foredeck, suggesting that he stick to preaching after this and leave the navigation to them.

2 Storm on the Mediterranean (27:14–38)

Verses 14–15—Upon rounding Cape Matala, jutting out of Crete at its mid south shore, they were suddenly struck by a violent wind from the east-northeast. After futile attempts to face in to the wind, the crew gave way to it and were driven southwestward across dangerously frothing swells.

Verse 16—Drifting 24 miles to the south, the voyagers ran under the protecting shelter of Cauda, a small island that cut their wind enough to let them hoist up and secure the huge waterlogged lifeboat they had been towing. Waves were likely breaking over that boat and swamping it. Or, if not, the winds might have caused it to swing dangerously close to the hull of their ship. Verse 17—They also used the relatively calmer waters to reinforce the ship, dropping cables under the hull in a U-shaped fashion and then tightening both ends of the cables at center deck.

Once they left the protection of Cauda, the northeaster could have driven them down onto the Syrtes—dangerous shoals off the North African coast. So they lowered their gear, lashing down on deck the sails and rigging except for some small storm sail to keep rudder control for a westerly course as the ship was driven before the wind.

Verse 18—The next day, however, they lost all shelter from Crete and found themselves in the center of a seething Mediterranean tempest, which howled with relentless fury. The pitching and rolling tore pieces of the cargo loose, and they were banging from one side of the hull to the other. Quickly, the crew pitched the loose freight overboard. Verse 19—The next day, since the battered ship was taking on some water, they threw overboard even the ship's furniture and whatever tackle could be spared to lighten the vessel.

Verse 20—For more than 10 days the storm screamed on and, without sun by day or stars by night, they had no bearings to fix their position. Eventually, the nauseated, terrified passengers lost all hope of surviving, and—even more horrifying—so did the captain and crew. Verse 21—At that worst moment Paul gathered them together and said (with a predictable opener), "Men, you should have taken my advice not to sail from Crete; then you would have spared yourselves this damage and loss." The poor ship owner, who had been watching his investment diminish by the hour, must have agreed!

But Paul had more to his message than "I-told-you-so" slogans. He made an astonishing statement: Verses 22–26—"But now I urge you to keep up your courage, because not one of you will be lost; only the ship will be destroyed. Last night an angel of the God whose I am and whom I serve stood beside me and said, 'Do not be afraid, Paul. You must stand trial before Caesar; and God has graciously given you the lives of all who sail with you.' So keep up your courage, men, for I have faith in God that it will happen just as He told me. Nevertheless, we must run aground on some island."

Verses 27–28—On the fourteenth night of the storm, the sailors suspected that land was near, probably from the roar of nearby surf. They took a sounding and found 20 fathoms of depth. Then, several moments later, they measured 15 fathoms. Verse 29—Rushing to the stern, they threw out four anchors to hold the ship off any rocks ahead. When the anchors finally caught on the sea bottom, it marked the first time since Crete that captain and crew had the ship under general control.

Verse 30—Squinting in the darkness, the crew saw either surf or points of lamplight in the distance. Could it be land? Word raced along the deck, and soon the crew was lowering the great lifeboat to escape the ship. But Paul caught them in the act.

They made up a story about laying out anchors from the bow, but Paul knew it was a lie. Verse 31—Calling Julius, he said, "Unless these men stay with the ship, you cannot be saved." Verse 32—Now with implicit faith in Paul's judgment, the centurion had his men cut away the ropes of the lifeboat and set it adrift, sacrificing their one avenue of escape.

Verses 33–38—Near dawn, Paul addressed passengers and crew, urging them to eat something, as he himself promptly did, giving thanks to God. He thereby set a worthy example, whatever the crisis. The passengers followed Paul's advice, heartened at last by the landfall nearby. Then they lightened the ship still more, throwing the remaining wheat cargo into the sea, some of which they had been saving for food. The lighter the ship, the farther it could sail toward shore before scraping sea bottom.

3 Shipwreck at Malta (27:39–44)

Verses 39–42—When day broke, they saw a bay with a beach dead ahead. Hoisting their foresail, they untied the two steering oars on each side of the stern in order to steer the ship. Then they cut away their anchors and scudded before the still-blowing northeaster until their bow finally rammed into a shoal at the head of the bay and stuck fast. When the pounding surf started breaking up the stern, the Roman guards drew out their swords to kill the prisoners, lest any swim off and escape.

Verses 43–44—Julius, however, vetoed this customary procedure, because he trusted Paul—his predictions had proven deadly accurate—and he did not wish Paul cut down with the others. Instead, Julius told all who could swim to plunge into the water and make for shore, while others should float in on planks and debris from the ship. Venturing overboard as ordered, they were pulled out of the swirling surf and onto the beach by friendly natives. Only then did they learn that they had landed on Malta, the small island between Sicily and Africa. It was only eight miles wide and 18 miles long, but it was better than any lifeboat.

That all 276 people on shipboard should have been saved in such a fashion may seem incredible.

But a visit to that landfall today near the northern tip of Malta suggests that "St. Paul's Shoal" within "St. Paul's Bay" are sites not only correctly named, but so near surrounding shores that loss of life could indeed have been prevented, especially with friendly Maltese wading out to assist them.

Conclusion

And so the question—how would Paul's faith stand up in a crisis that threatened his very life—is answered so very easily. Here was a man, marked by the Master, who could soften hardened guards on shipboard, do some shrewd weather forecasting, inspire courage in crisis, build faith where there was total despair, and thus save 276 lives that would have been lost to the angry Mediterranean. If Christians are to be "little Christs" to their neighbors, Paul surely fulfilled that role on this voyage. As Jesus stilled the tempest on the Sea of Galilee and saved the Twelve, so Paul, by God's grace and guidance, helped save the 276 on the Mediterranean. There is no end to what God in His grace can accomplish.

So, too, God is at work in *our* lives. In the midst of broken relationships, financial losses, and temptations of every kind, we can know that our loving God is with us, and that "in all things" He "works for the good of those who love Him" (Romans 8:28).

"He who did not spare His own Son, but gave Him up for us all—how will He not also, along with Him, graciously give us all things?" (Romans 8:32).

Concluding Activities

Speak a brief prayer, thanking God for His protection and blessing upon participants as they continue to serve Him and be His witnesses in this world. Then make any necessary announcements and distribute study leaflet 9.

The Gospel Comes to Rome

Acts 28

Preparing for the Session

Central Focus

After wintering on Malta (where Paul demonstrated the power of Jesus by healing many sick people), Paul was taken on to Rome, where he was welcomed by Christians already there and proclaimed the Gospel to Rome's Jewish leaders.

Objectives

That participants, led by the Holy Spirit, will

1. understand better how and why the Holy Spirit gave powerful testimony to the truth of the Gospel of Jesus by working through Paul in performing miraculous signs;
2. be more confident that the Spirit will give power to their own witness concerning Jesus;
3. witness about Jesus more easily and readily as God provides opportunities.

Note for the small-group leaders: Lesson notes and other materials you will need begin on page 78.

Session Plan

Worship

As you lead the opening worship, refer again to Paul as a man of prayer during the mission travels we have studied in Acts. In addition to the record of his prayers in Acts, he gives us a glimpse of his prayer life in his epistles. In all his letters, Paul tells the congregations addressed that he always prays for them. You may want to read a few verses as examples, such as Philippians 1:3–6 or 1 Thessalonians 1:2–3.

Use the prayer in the study leaflet or a prayer of your own. As you pray, use the prayer posture of the week, palms open facing upward, resting on the lap. Share your experience of doing it according to the instructions in the study leaflet and let a few others share theirs, if there is time.

Introduce the hymn with a story of its author, Joseph Scriven. He was born in Ireland and immigrated to Ontario, where he taught school. He lived a life that modeled commitment to Jesus and dedication to service to others as a member of the Plymouth Brethren church. Yet his life was full of tragedy. His first fiancée drowned the night before the wedding. Years later his second fiancée died after a brief illness before they were married. He died at the age of 67, in failing health and deep depression. He wrote the hymn when he was 36 to send to his mother in Ireland to comfort her in a time of sorrow.

Hymn accompaniments are available in denominational hymnals, such as *Lutheran Worship* (refer to hymnal index). Note: Concordia Publishing House has available *Every Voice a Song*, a 9-CD set of organ accompaniments for 180 hymns and liturgy. All the initial worship hymns in the LifeLight courses are included in this resource. It's especially helpful for mission congregations and small parishes. See the list of study resources on page 6.

Devotion (optional)

Do you ever wish that your attempts to tell others about your faith in Jesus might be made with greater power or effect? Do you wish that the Holy Spirit would give you the ability to back up your statements of faith in some way so that those with whom you share your faith might be more impressed and know that it is really true? Do you ever wish that God would give you the power to heal miraculously or do some other miracle?

This week once again we read how God did powerfully back up Paul's witness about Jesus with miraculous powers. The venom of a deadly snake was unable to harm the apostle. Paul was able to heal miraculously many sick people on Malta.

God does such miraculous deeds when He Himself sees that they are needed to confirm His Word. God still can and does arrange for such miracles to happen. But God also has other ways of confirming the truth of His Word as it is proclaimed by Christians. The fact is that God does back up the witness you make, perhaps in ways that are unknown to you. We can be confident as we share the Gospel about Jesus with others, knowing that the God whose Gospel this is will accompany the Gospel we speak with power so that this Gospel has the desired effect. He may not do this in the same way He did it when Paul proclaimed the Gospel on Malta, but it is still God's Gospel, "the power of God for the salvation of everyone who believes" (Romans 1:16).

Lecture Presentation

Introduction

At last, Paul and his companions would approach the capital of the Roman Empire, the city to which he had addressed his greatest theological work, the Letter to the Romans. Finally, he would reach the destination he had targeted for many months, no, years. At Corinth he had written, "I planned many times to come to you [Roman Christians] (but have been prevented from doing so)" (Romans 1:13). And at the close of that same letter, he had also asked their prayers "so that by God's will I may come to you with joy and together with you be refreshed" (15:32). That prayer would now be answered: He was coming to them indeed, with joy (albeit also with a guard!), and he would surely be refreshed by them.

1 Wintering on Malta (28:1–10)

Verses 1–2—But, first, back to Malta, where Paul and his 275 shipmates were dragging themselves onto the beach where their ship had wrecked. Some of the islanders who rescued the victims of the shipwreck were busy building a bonfire on the beach to warm the survivors, since it was cold and rainy. Verses 3–6—Paul, ever helpful and hardworking, helped out by gathering a bundle of sticks and throwing them on the fire, when suddenly he felt a painful stinging in his hand. Fastened to it was an ugly viper, driven out of the twigs by the heat! Paul immediately shook the snake off his hand and into the flames.

Anyone else might have done the same, but would soon have suffered painful swelling, loss of consciousness, and then swift death, like Cleopatra of Egypt, who was bitten by the same species of asp viper. The Maltese assumed that Paul must have been a murderous criminal, marked by the gods for death despite his escape from shipwreck. But when Paul's arm was not swelling and he merely carried on without sign of punishment, the islanders changed their minds and decided Paul was a god!

Verses 7–9—Several miles south of that bonfire lay the estate of Publius, the "first [man] of the island," as the Greek has it, most probably the chief Roman magistrate on Malta. He generously played host to Paul and his companions for their first three days on the island.

Publius had a problem at home: his father lay ill with dysentery and fever. Yet when Paul prayed and laid his hands on the man, he was cured. Word of this spread quickly across Malta, and Paul soon had a busy ministry of healing during the three months they wintered on the island.

Verse 10—Any further progress toward Rome would have to await the new sailing season in early March. There could be no better proof of the success of Paul's ministry on Malta than the warm appreciation lavished on the apostle and his party when they finally did prepare to set sail in March. Paul and his party were accorded honors, as well as "the supplies we needed" aboard ship.

Doubtless, Publius himself and his family led the cheers at wharfside. We never hear of Publius again. The later church father Jerome records a tradition that Publius was not only converted (not surprising), but that he was also martyred for his faith (doubtful). The persecution that Nero would soon unleash on the church was largely limited to Rome.

Rather, Publius was only another in the long line of personalities touched by Paul of Tarsus on the catastrophic voyage to Rome. Living out the faith he preached, Paul had a touch that was always a blessing, always a help, sometimes a healing, or even physical salvation itself.

2 The Voyage to Italy (28:11–15)

Winter on the treacherous Mediterranean—the only

time it really was treacherous—had now passed. The almond trees were budding into bloom. Winds now caressed rather than killed, and they were wafting gently from southerly directions. The sea lanes were reliable once again, and ships in port all over that body of water the Romans called "Our Sea" now prepared to set sail, including the vessel at Malta on which Julius and his famous prisoner were now embarking. It would be the final voyage ever recorded for St. Paul. (He *may* have taken more, but we have no record of them.)

Verses 11–13—In late February or early March of A.D. 58 or 59—New Testament chronology is still not absolute—Paul and his company, as well as a probable majority of the shipwreck survivors, set sail on the good ship *Twin Brothers*, another great Alexandrian grain ship that had wintered at Malta. It was named for the pagan gods Castor and Pollux, who were adorning its prow as wooden figureheads. This time their brief voyage was simple and easily traceable, as they put in at Syracuse near the tip of Sicily and then at Rhegium on the toe of the Italian boot.

There they waited for a reliable south wind to carry them through the Straits of Messina without foundering on the rock and whirlpool there. When a spring breeze developed, they easily ran with it through the Straits, up along the western coast of Italy, and into the Bay of Naples.

Gliding past Capri toward evening, they saw the breast-shaped hulk of Mount Vesuvius lording it over the eastern shore of the bay. In just 20 years, it would rumble into life and bury the towns of Herculaneum and Pompeii, nestled near its base, in a cataclysm of mud, lava, and fiery ash. Now the *Twin Brothers* reached its destination, the commercial port of Puteoli on the north shore of the Bay of Naples. Today it is called Pozzuoli, and ruins of the *macellum* or covered market hall there are all that remain of one of the first buildings Paul would have seen after landing, since it faces the waterfront.

Christians were already established at Puteoli—Paul's fame had preceded him there—and the missionaries were invited to stay with them for a time. Verse 14—In an extraordinary concession Julius allowed Paul a week in Puteoli, unquestionably a favor in return for his crucial services on the shipwreck voyage. It may be from this early congregation that the faith expanded around the Bay of Naples, because there were Christians in nearby Herculaneum shortly afterward. One of the houses in that resort town, today excavated out of its lava burial by Mount Vesuvius, shows the clear outlines of a metal cross that had been embedded in the wall over a charred kneeler in an upstairs room. The cross evidently is just as old a Christian symbol as the fish.

Verse 15—The final leg of Paul's journey was beautiful in the early Italian spring. Soon their highway merged with the famous Appian Way, the busy artery that led them northward to Rome. At the forty-third milestone on that road (meaning exactly 43 miles from a column erected in the Roman Forum), Luke identified a way station called Forum of Appius. Both here and also 10 miles farther on at a village named Three Taverns, Paul and his party were happily surprised to find welcoming delegations from the Christians of Rome. The church there had been alerted to Paul's arrival, and possibly many of the people named in Romans 16 were clustered along the sides of the Appian Way in a grand welcoming committee. What enormously cheered Paul and his companions must have astonished Julius, the centurion.

3 Paul's Proclamation in Rome (28:16–28)

Verse 16—At last they reached the sprawling capital of the Mediterranean world, Paul's greatest goal for the Gospel. Julius delivered his prisoners there, as well as the documents of indictment on them. He may well have had a few generous things to say about Paul to the commandant, for Luke adds that after registering, "Paul was allowed to live by himself, with a soldier [not Julius] to guard him"—doubtless near the Praetorian Camp in northeastern Rome.

Verses 17–20—Only three days elapsed between the close of Paul's momentous journey and his resumption of mission work. Barely settled, he invited the local Jewish leaders to meet with him at his rented abode. There was a large Jewish colony in Rome at this time. Aquila and Priscilla, Paul's co-workers in Corinth, had come from this community, and had evidently returned (since Paul had sent them greetings at Romans 16:3). Very possibly they had led the delegation of welcome at the Forum of Appius.

When the Jewish leaders had gathered, Paul candidly

introduced himself, his faith, and his mission, finally summing it all up in one brilliant sentence: "It is because of the hope of Israel that I am bound with this chain"—fettered for the faith, chained for Christ—the messianic hope of Israel ... and of everyone else.

Verses 21–22—"We have not received any letters from Judea concerning you," the Jewish leaders replied, "and none of the brothers who have come from there has reported or said anything bad about you. But ... we know that people everywhere are talking against this sect." This is a remarkable statement: it shows that the "sect" of Christianity had indeed penetrated Rome some years earlier and was causing some commotion in many of the synagogues there. But Paul himself was an unknown quantity to the Roman Jews at this time. Clearly, the Jerusalem authorities had either tired of prosecuting his case or had lost interest in it. Otherwise they would surely have alerted their comrades in Rome.

Verse 23—Open-mindedly, the leaders of the Jewish synagogues at Rome decided to hear Paul further and agreed with him on a day when they would bring their members in to hear him. At the appointed time, they came to his lodging in large numbers. In perhaps his ultimate effort to Christianize the Jews, Paul lectured all day long on Jesus as the fulfillment of the Law and the Prophets. Verse 24—The response was quite similar to what the apostle had encountered almost everywhere else on his mission journeys: some believed, while oth ers—probably a majority—did not.

Verses 25–29—As they were leaving, Paul invoked Judaism's greatest prophet, Isaiah, to condemn the dullness of their senses in not perceiving the true Messiah. He said, in effect, that their very unbelief was a fulfillment of Isaiah 6:9–10. Wistfully, he concluded: "Therefore I want you to know that God's salvation has been sent to the Gentiles, and they will listen!"

4 The Close of Acts (28:30–31)

Verse 30—Luke, who was clearly present on this occasion, closes the scene—and also the Book of Acts—with the following intriguing verse: "For two whole years Paul stayed there in his own rented house and welcomed all who came to see him. Boldly and without hindrance he preached the kingdom of God and taught about the Lord Jesus Christ."

What happened then, Luke? Why did Paul have to wait two years for his hearing or trial before Nero? What was Paul's fate? Peter's? Yours, for that matter? What about the great fire of Rome that destroyed much of the city just three years after you break off your account? And why did Nero persecute the Christians so horribly after that fire? And ...

No serious student of the New Testament has failed to fire these queries at the beloved physician and friend of Paul. Luke's conclusion of the Book of Acts has been explained in various ways. Some have speculated that Luke wrote an as-yet-undiscovered 2 Acts, and many biblical scholars dream of someday finding an ancient scroll that would begin, "This third treatise, O Theophilus ..." (That gentleman, of course, was the man to whom Luke had addressed both his Gospel and the Acts. Theophilus may have been an unknown Roman official or possibly any "friend of God," as his Greek name translates.)

But the conclusion of Acts is, in fact, honest and satisfactory after all, because Luke's great purpose was only to show how the Gospel had spread from Jerusalem to Rome (Acts 1:8). He certainly did just that, and with distinction.

5 Paul's Last Years

Of all religious beliefs in the world, past or present, none have more thoroughly based themselves on history than Judaism and Christianity. For that reason, it is possible to use the tools and sources of ancient history to give answers to some of the nagging questions we just posed to Luke. Let us try to answer as many as we can.

Why did Paul have to wait two years for his trial before Nero? Simply because Nero was *not* in Rome at the time to hear his case, and the reason for that is quite extraordinary. *Very* near the time that Paul's ship was gliding into the Bay of Naples in March of 59 Nero had just arranged to have his mother murdered.

On the evening of March 20 he gave a banquet in her honor at his villa on the western rim of the same Bay of Naples and then saw her off at his dock for a short cruise across the bay to the villa where she was staying. Unfortunately, her boat was nothing less than a collapsible cabin cruiser, rigged by Nero and his associates so that levers would open the hull and scuttle the ship.

But the plot failed. Hinges on the hull trap door had been mounted on the wrong side, opening *outward* against the water pressure! Meanwhile, Nero's mother saved herself by diving off the ship and swimming in the bay until she was rescued by some oyster fishermen, who brought her safely back to her villa on shore. By dawn, however, a detail of Nero's marines stormed into the villa and clubbed her to death anyway, as she lay in her bed. Nero then grew so worried at how the people of Rome would react to the murder of his own mother that he did not return to his capital for many months—hence the delay in Paul's hearing.

How was Paul's case before Nero decided? The hearing also had to wait until Paul's accusers arrived from Judea—if they went to the effort of making the trip. His chief prosecutor, the high priest Ananias, had been deposed, and Ananias's successor may not have been interested in the case. Paul's opponents in Palestine, then, could achieve much more by doing nothing at all, for this would leave their target in a peculiar legal limbo. Still, there is little doubt that Paul finally did face Nero himself for trial, because God had told Paul that he would stand before Caesar (Acts 27:24).

What probably happened is that one of Paul's more powerful Roman friends pressed the case for him, and Paul eventually had his day in court. Some Jewish or Roman substitute prosecutor would have raised the three original charges first lodged against Paul at Caesarea by Tertullus (24:1–8). For his part, Paul would have offered a by now predictable defense, including the episode on the Damascus road, which might have made the superstitious Nero a bit uncomfortable. And although Nero had murdered his mother and his list of crimes was growing, he had not yet reached the stage of immorality and cruelty associated with his later reign. Accordingly, with Paul's eloquence and Agrippa II's statement on his behalf on the one hand, and the less-than-impressive charges on the other, Nero may indeed have acquitted the apostle. At this point, the Roman state had not yet declared Christianity illegal.

Although some important scholars disagree, there is strong, though not absolutely conclusive, evidence that Paul actually *was* acquitted after his first trial at Rome and that he subsequently visited both Spain in the West (see Romans 15:28) and his beloved mission churches in the East. The pastoral epistles—1 and 2 Timothy and Titus—cannot be fitted satisfactorily into the three mission journeys, and they tell of Paul's later activities in the Aegean world. Clement of Rome and other early church fathers also confirm his mission to Spain.

If he did visit Spain, Paul would next have returned eastward to confirm the faithful in a "fourth mission journey" to the Aegean. Titus refers to Paul's work on the island of Crete, and the other pastoral epistles have him back in Greece and then Asia Minor. There, probably because of a dispute with a certain Alexander the coppersmith (2 Timothy 4:14), he was arrested a second time and sent to face Nero once again. Now, about A.D. 66–67, Paul would have been in mortal danger at Rome, whatever the charges that had brought him there. Two years earlier, Nero, in deflecting from himself the public outcry that he had set fire to Rome, blamed the Christians for arson and tortured them to death. Being a Christian now carried the death penalty, so Nero or his justices could hardly acquit this strange and troublesome *leader* of the Christians.

This time Paul had no illusions about being set free. When his last day had come, the apostle was presumably accompanied in his final journey across Rome to the Ostian Gate by a grieving group of friends who had survived the cruel first wave of persecution. Several miles beyond the Gate, on the road to the port of Ostia, stood the chopping block. While the sword was being prepared by the executioner (Roman citizens were not crucified), Paul doubtless made a last statement. His words were very probably similar to what he had written earlier to his young co-worker, Timothy: "The time has come for my departure. I have fought the good fight, I have finished the race, I have kept the faith. Now there is in store for me the crown of righteousness, which the Lord, the righteous Judge, will award to me on that day—and not only to me, but also to all who have longed for His appearing" (2 Timothy 4:6–8).

The blade dropped, the apostle died—the greatest missionary, the greatest theologian in the history of Christianity, and—above all—the one who had universalized its message.

Sustained by the hope of the resurrection that was the centerpiece of all his preaching, Paul's friends must then have buried him nearby, along the Ostian Way. The much-traveled apostle would have appreciated that gesture—burial alongside a highway. Today the road connects Rome with her international airport at Ostia.

And whatever happened to Luke and the apostles? After remaining at Paul's side and tending to any of his medical needs, Luke finished the Gospel named for him, as well as the Book of Acts. Then he labored in Bithynia, where he died at age 74, "full of the Holy Spirit," according to one early church tradition. Peter was most likely martyred in some connection with Nero's persecution at Rome. John, "the disciple whom Jesus loved," carried his ministry to Ephesus, according to early Christian tradition, where he also acted as dutiful foster son to Mary, the mother of Jesus, a role assigned to him at Calvary. Peter's brother Andrew went to the north shore of the Black Sea—Scythia then, Ukraine today; Thaddaeus preached in Syria and Armenia; Bartholomew and Thomas in Persia and India. Barnabas missionized the islands, while his cousin Mark, later happily reconciled with Paul, wrote his Gospel in Rome. Others worked elsewhere: this list is not complete.

Conclusion

Even though the second half of Luke's fascinating record in Acts has focused almost entirely on Paul of Tarsus, the other apostles, then, were also doing their part to fulfill the Great Commission in Matthew 28. Like Paul, all endured daunting hardships for the faith, many suffering martyrdom. Not one of them could see the ultimate triumph of Christianity except through the eyes of faith and the inspiration of the same Holy Spirit who had arrived on that extraordinary Pentecost and had never withdrawn. Though at the time the Christian cause seemed persecuted, burned, crucified, beheaded, and even eaten out of existence by the greatest power in the world, a greater power was at work that would see Christianity conquer Rome a little more than two centuries later, and "the ends of the earth" after that, in Jesus' own prediction.

It was Christ, not Caesar, who captured the future. Every one of the one billion Christians in the world today should be grateful to Luke and his gifted pen for telling us how the most successful enterprise in all of history began its spiritual conquest of the Mediterranean—and the globe.

His record remains an inspiration for the church today, which is only an extension of the Book of Acts across 20 centuries, completing Luke's account, in a sense. Believers should have no trouble identifying with the ordeals facing the apostles—we have our own ordeals today—or with their triumphs—we also have our successes. The same God animates both the past and the present. If we can enter our own names into a spiritual book titled "Acts of the Holy Spirit This Year," then our LifeLight series on the "Acts of the Apostles" will have achieved its aim.

Concluding Activities

End with a brief prayer, thanking God for the blessings received in this course. Make any necessary announcements (including information about the next LifeLight course) and—if your schedule so suggests—distribute the first study sheet of the next LifeLight course.

Small-Group Leaders Material

A Step toward World Evangelization (Paul's First Mission Journey)

Acts 13–14

Preparing for the Session

Central Focus

The Holy Spirit calls Paul and Barnabas to take the Gospel into Asia Minor, as the Gospel continues to move from Jerusalem to the ends of the earth.

Objectives

That participants, led by the Holy Spirit, will

1. possess a more complete understanding of how the Holy Spirit caused the Gospel to be spread from Jerusalem to the ends of the earth;
2. become more confident in their own witness of the Gospel to others;
3. be encouraged as they see and experience conflicts among "erring and faithful" Christians;
4. be better able to meet and respond to opposition to the Gospel;
5. praise God for the growth of the church.

Small-Group Discussion Helps

Day 1 • Acts 13:1–12

As you begin the study of the second half of the Book of Acts, be sensitive to any new members of the class who may not have been with the group for the previous course on Acts 1–12. This first assignment will make a connection with the first half of Acts and put both parts of the book in the context of the mission command of Jesus and the purpose of the writer, St. Luke, to record the spread of the Gospel from Jerusalem to Rome.

1. Finding Jerusalem, Judea, and Samaria on a map of the Holy Land will show how the Gospel was spread outward from Jerusalem. When the Gospel reached Antioch, it had spread throughout the Holy Land and beyond. (a) The Holy Spirit directed the congregation at Antioch of Syria (we shall soon come across another Antioch, in Pisidia) to commission and send Saul (Paul) and Barnabas on a mission journey that would take them and the Gospel westward. (b) Acts 11:20–21 tells us that a large segment—probably the great majority—of the congregation at Antioch was Gentile (non-Jewish).

2. Agabus was one of the prophets who went from Jerusalem to Antioch. God used him to foretell a famine that would affect the entire Roman Empire (Acts 11:27–28). Agabus may have left Antioch, since he is not mentioned in the list of five. The primary function of the five was to proclaim the Gospel and to teach the Gentiles the Word of God. The three who were not chosen by God as foreign missionaries probably continued their ministry in Antioch.

3. We have the promise that the Spirit will help us as we witness to Christ, even giving us the words to speak. Also, as we meditate in our hearts on what "Jesus means to me," we more readily find the words to share the Good News in a winsome and meaningful way.

4. Fasting for religious purposes continues to be practiced, though not as widely as previously. Some participants can share experiences of fasting on Sunday before going to Communion, fasting during Lent by giving up meat or some special food, or fasting on a retreat or special time of renewal. Probably, however, participants will suggest other ways by which they attempt to focus themselves on prayer and meditation—choosing a quiet time or place, establishing regular devotional habits.

5. Let the class share their thoughts. Expect answers like these: Barnabas may have wanted to share the Gospel with his family and friends or may have had contacts on Cyprus; Paul may have wanted to start in a new place. Whatever our speculation, we know that the Holy Spirit directed them.

6. The name *Paul* would help him be accepted in a Roman world.

7. Both the miracle and message influenced Sergius Paulus. At first he may have heard about the preaching of Barnabas and Saul and that many were following them, so he wanted to hear about it (v. 7). Then he was impressed by the authority and power God had given Paul over the evil in Elymas.

Day 2 • Acts 13:13–43

8. Paul called John Mark's return home a desertion (Acts 15:37–39). He didn't want John Mark to lose courage again and leave them without the help they needed.

9. Disagreements and conflicts are all too common among us in the church today. They are also part of the experience of the apostles. But such conflicts can be overcome and relationships reknit. That this happened in the case of Paul, John Mark, and Barnabas should be encouraging to us.

10. Paul went first to the synagogue and sought permission to speak to the congregation during their Sabbath worship.

11. There were two types of converts or proselytes to the Jewish faith: proselytes of the gate, who observed the general moral code of the Jews but were not circumcised, and proselytes of righteousness, who were complete converts accepting circumcision and the full Law of Moses. There were many such proselytes mingled with the Jews in Paul's day. Both were present on Pentecost (Acts 2:10) and in the synagogues where Paul preached. As Paul begins his sermon (v. 16), he addresses both the "men of Israel" and "you Gentiles." In verse 26 he refers to "God-fearing Gentiles." This term may refer to the first type of proselyte or Gentile convert, while "devout converts to Judaism" (v. 43) may refer to the second type. In any event, Paul reached some Gentiles by preaching in synagogues, and through these he probably had access to their Gentile friends and relatives.

12. The sermon divisions are (I) verses 15–25; (II) verses 26–36; (III) verses 37–41. Allow participants time to share their impressions of the sermon.

Day 3 • Acts 13:44–52

13. Jealousy, though sometimes appropriate, most often is a product of selfishness and our sinful human nature. It often fosters envy, sinful pride, and resentfulness. When jealousy crops up among Christians, it can result in factions and a party spirit that inhibits and may even prevent Christian love and sharing the Gospel with others.

14.(a) Let the class repeat the words they put in the blanks and then discuss the purpose of their light, to shine so that others may see it, to come to know their Father in Jesus Christ, and to give Him glory. Words to be placed in the blanks are *the world; Jews, Gentiles; world; let the world (all people) see and glorify God.* (b) As time permits, let volunteers share their responses. Some may volunteer evidence they've seen in the lives of fellow participants.

15. As Paul points out, someone must communicate the Gospel before it can be believed and bring salvation. Every Christian is to be a witness who shares the Gospel with those who do not yet believe it. Some will be reached most effectively by each one of us.

16. See the comments on question 11 mentioned previously for a description of the two types of proselytes. Some might question how these women could have such influence in the city. Perhaps they were persons with wealth, or they may have been married to important men. In any case their opposition, along with that of the city's male leaders, was finally effective, and Paul and Barnabas were expelled. Jesus told His disciples to shake the dust from their feet when they were not accepted on their preaching tours. In addition to Luke 9:5, see Mark 6:11. The disciples were even told to wipe off the dust that sticks to their feet (Luke 10:11). Jesus said that this was a "testimony against them" (Mark 6:11), a mark of separation from those who reject the Gospel.

17. **Challenge question**. Do not expect everyone in the class to have completed this challenge question, but allow those who did to share. The blanks in the references are (a) power to be witnesses for Jesus; (b) the disciples spoke the Word with boldness; (c) the deacons were known for their wisdom; (d) faith is connected with the Holy Spirit. (e) As participants discuss their own lives, emphasize that the focus of the Acts passages is on sharing the Gospel so that others might come to know Jesus Christ as Savior. That is the work of the Holy Spirit through us today.

Day 4 • Acts 14:1–20

18. (a) Many Jews and Gentiles believed at Iconium, an important city of Galatia that Paul used as his base to reach into the surrounding area. (b) God backed up the preaching of the apostles by enabling them to do miraculous signs and wonders. (c) The Gospel was spread to Lystra and Derbe and the surrounding countryside.

19. **Challenge question**. The similar items (with both A and B) are *congenital lameness, unsolicited healing,* and *two evangelists involved.* The rest are dissimilar items: The Jerusalem beggar was a Jew and had no faith (A). All he wanted from Peter and John was a handout of money. The Lystra lame man was a Gentile who had probably heard Paul preach and had faith to anticipate a healing (B). God is the only power that heals. He chooses where he heals, when He heals, and whom He heals—some people with faith and some without.

20.(a) Have someone in the class read aloud the list of Paul's sufferings in 2 Corinthians 11:23–26. Notice how specific he is as to the number of times each thing happened. (b) In the Sermon on the Mount (Matthew 5:11–12), Jesus said that those who are persecuted are blessed and so should rejoice. In Matthew 5:44 He directs disciples to love their enemies and pray for those who persecute them. (c) Let the class share the kinds of persecution they may have experienced, such as rejection; ridicule; being considered old-fashioned, bizarre, or strange.

21. (a) At Lystra (Acts 14:15–17) Paul emphasized that God is the Creator of earth and sea, the giver of rain and seasons, and the provider of food. Paul used natural theology with the Gentiles to open the way for the message of God's grace in Jesus Christ. (b) We also must start where people are when we share the Gospel with them. Some people may have no knowledge of the Bible and little, if any, knowledge of who God is or what He is really like. We must sometimes start with the basics.

Day 5 • Acts 14:21–28

22. *Disciples* emphasizes that we are followers of Jesus who are always learning from His teaching in the Scriptures and are growing in our knowledge and our application of Christian principles. *Brothers* emphasizes our relationship to fellow Christians, a relationship of love that flows from and is modeled after our relationship with Jesus. *Christian* emphasizes that we worship Christ, belong to Him, and reflect Him in our attitudes and behavior.

23. We can hear mission reports in our congregation, attend mission festivals, read mission reports in our periodicals, and correspond with missionaries. All such things will give us joy as we hear how the Gospel is being spread and souls are being won for Christ.

24. You may hear comments about the way Barnabas and Saul were chosen, the active opposition by the Jewish leaders, the eagerness of the Gentiles to believe, and such.

Agreeing That All Nations Are Included (The Apostolic Council of Jerusalem)

Acts 15

Preparing for the Session

Central Focus

The assembled leaders of the church affirm and declare the fundamental principle of the Gospel that salvation is through faith in Christ alone, without keeping the laws of the old covenant.

Objectives

That participants, led by the Holy Spirit, will

1. understand more clearly the Gospel principle that salvation is by faith in Christ alone, without the works of the Law;
2. become more confident of salvation through faith alone;
3. be unswayed by claims that they must do something besides trust in Christ to be saved;
4. in Christian freedom and love avoid offending those who are weaker in faith or who are still under the burden of erring consciences.

Small-Group Discussion Helps

Day 1 • Acts 15:1–11

1. The group of teachers who insisted that the Gentiles could not be saved without being circumcised were reacting to the reports of Paul's success in establishing Gentile churches. Antioch was the mother of the Gentile churches, so they began there. The church wanted counsel from the leaders, the apostles, and so sent their delegation. (a) When Peter first confronted this attitude, he was charged with going into the home of the Gentile Cornelius and eating with Gentiles food that was not kosher (ceremonially clean). God had to convince Peter with a vision that the Gentiles were to be accepted, although Peter still had trouble with this (Galatians 2:11–14). (b) Christ was the mediator of the new covenant promised by Jeremiah. It was established by the shedding of His blood to pay for the sins of the world and make reconciliation with God. The ceremonies and laws of the Old Testament pointed to the fulfillment of God's plan in Jesus.

2. (a) Verses 1, 5: The men from Judea, believers of the party of the Pharisees. These were probably Jews who were Pharisees before they came to faith, as was Paul. (b) Verse 2: Paul, Barnabas, and other believers from the church in Antioch who were the appointed delegates. (c) Verse 6: The apostles and elders, who were leaders of the church in Jerusalem and who managed the meetings. The elders were probably pastors. Some think there were three meetings: (1) a general meeting for receiving the delegates and hearing reports, (vv. 4–5); (2) a meeting of the leaders to discuss the issue on the agenda (vv. 6–11); and (3) a general meeting of the entire assembly to hear the leaders' recommendation and to make a decision (vv. 12–22).

3. (a) Brothers, church, believers, and disciples. (b) The terms suggest that they accepted everyone who confessed Jesus as their Messiah with love and respect. They were united in their faith and committed to their purpose of sharing the Good News with the world.

4. (a) The terms used, "God ... accepted" (v. 8), "no distinction" (v. 9), and "through ... grace" (v. 11), stress the truth of Ephesians 2:8–9 that salvation is entirely by grace through faith. (b) Encourage the class to share statements of why they accept other people; but be prepared to hear some expressions of reluctance or difficulty in doing so.

Day 2 • Acts 15:12–21

5. When Paul told the congregations in Phoenicia and Samaria that God was converting the Gentiles, the "news made all the brothers very glad" (v. 3). At the assembly of believers in Jerusalem when Barnabas and Paul told about the "miraculous signs and wonders" among the Gentiles, the gathering was "silent as they listened" (v. 12). Notice that Barnabas is mentioned first in this account, perhaps because he was better known in Jerusalem than Paul. As the angels in heaven rejoice over one sinner who repents, so we rejoice over every person who believes and confesses Jesus Christ as Lord (Luke 15:10).

6. In Acts 21:18 Paul reports directly to James, the recognized leader of the church. Paul mentions James as the first of the three pillars of the church, James, Peter, and John (Galatians 2:9). This James cannot be the brother of John and disciple of Jesus because that James was beheaded by Herod (Acts 12:2). This James is rather the "Lord's brother" (Galatians 1:19), perhaps the oldest brother (after Jesus) since he is mentioned

first among the brothers of Jesus in Matthew 13:55.

7. The church in Jerusalem was sensitive to the Gentiles' weakness for immorality and the Jewish sensitivity to anything connected with idol worship and contrary to the laws of Moses. When Paul speaks about similar issues in Romans and Corinthians, he is (a) concerned about offending the weak and causing them to stumble and sin and about making every effort to foster peace in the church. (b) A weak conscience that believes in the existence of pagan gods is defiled by eating food sacrificed to them. In this case food, which has no positive spiritual value, would actually weaken faith.

8. **Challenge question**. Because of the teaching of Jesus, the testimony of the Old Testament, and the witness of Peter, it was accepted that the Gentiles were part of the Kingdom, without strings attached. The four recommendations are suggestions for peace in the church rather than laws. (a) Verse 29 identifies the food. It is polluted because it was sacrificed to heathen gods. Paul says that to knowingly eat such food is wrong since it was food offered to demons, who were the real identity behind the nonexistent pagan gods. (b) Paul tells the Corinthians that their bodies were bought by Jesus' blood and belonged to God, so their bodies were to bring Him honor. Sexual immorality dishonors God's property, the body. (c) The reason for refraining from eating animals that were strangled is the same as the reason for not eating blood. Jews butchered their animals in a way that allowed the blood to drain out of the meat. God told his people not to eat blood, since life is in the blood. The blood-life belonged to God and was to be offered to Him in sacrifices. Also this prohibition pointed to the ultimate sacrifice, that of Jesus, and to the atonement His death would accomplish (Hebrews 9:11–14, 22).

Day 3 • Acts 15:22–29

9. Verses 6–11 probably describe a separate meeting of the apostles and elders to consider the question (v. 6). On the basis of that discussion, James made his proposal, a customary thing for leaders to do. (a) In verse 22, at the selection of the representatives to go to Antioch, the three groups mentioned are the apostles, elders, and the whole church. (b) The Holy Spirit (v. 28) was behind the decision that was made: "it seemed good to the Holy Spirit and to us." (c) Church leaders today may take encouragement in the role that the Spirit takes in the life of the church, particularly in decisions that affect the work of the Gospel.

10. **Challenge question**. In verse 19 James used the phrase "not make it difficult," while Peter asked in verse 10 why they "try to test God by putting on the necks of the disciples a yoke." Today Christians need to be concerned lest we lay upon new Christians requirements that are not listed in the Bible and that are not necessary for bearing witness to the Gospel. As time permits, let participants discuss possibilities or actual experiences.

11. (a) Joseph Barsabbas (Acts 1:23) was one of the two selected by the early church as a candidate to replace Judas. He must have been a respected leader, as was Matthias, who was then elected. In verse 22 these men are described as our "own men" and as "leaders among the brothers." In verse 32 they are called "prophets." Their task was to "confirm by word of mouth" (v. 27), as well as to "encourage and strengthen" the disciples in Antioch (v. 32). (b) These men were chosen and commissioned by the church for their task, while the first group of teachers who went to Antioch did so "without ... authorization" (v. 24).

Day 4 • Acts 15:22–35

12. Prior to this point the references are to "Jesus" or "Lord" or "the Christ." Now they are put together in the expression "Lord Jesus Christ." The early confession of faith was simply "Jesus is Lord," but in more formal circumstances the full expression was used, "Lord Jesus Christ." Encourage participants to say how they view Jesus as their Lord, who rules in their lives with His love and grace.

13. The response in the church at Antioch is reflected in words like "glad for its encouraging message" (v. 31), "encourage and strengthen" (v. 32), "blessing of peace" (v. 33).

14. The message from the church in Jerusalem, together with the teaching and preaching of Paul and Silas, resulted in the churches being strengthened in faith, and they "grew daily in numbers" (16:5). The Holy Spirit creates faith through the Gospel that results in growth, but He uses people like Paul and Silas to deliver the message and occasions like the letter from Jerusalem to prepare the way.

15. **Challenge question.** In Galatians 2:1–10 Paul summarizes the convention in Jerusalem, and then in verses 11–16 he describes a visit by Peter to Antioch. Evidently the original Judaizers, or the party of Pharisees, were not stopped by the letter from the Jerusalem convention. Here they are called the "circumcision group." Peter was intimidated by them and separated himself from the Gentiles. Other Jews followed his example, including Barnabas. (a) Paul calls this hypocrisy, not acting in line with the truth of the Gospel, forcing Gentiles to follow Jewish customs. (b) The important truth that Paul states is that we are justified before God not by our good deeds, but only through faith in Jesus Christ.

(c) This truth is the heart of the Gospel. We cannot be saved by being circumcised or keeping any Jewish customs but only by faith in Jesus Christ. That is why He came, died, and rose again.

Day 5 • Acts 15:36–41

16. As Paul concluded his first mission journey, he retraced his steps in order to visit the churches he had started in Lystra, Iconium, and Antioch (Acts 14:21–22), "strengthening the disciples and encouraging them to remain true to the faith." The two obstacles to their faith were the persecution prompted by the Jews and the false teachers. Whenever Paul visited congregations, he sought to strengthen them in the faith, as he did when going through Syria and Cilicia (15:41), and when he delivered the letter from Jerusalem (16:4). (a) Paul suggested to Barnabas that they "go back and visit the brothers in all the towns where we preached the word of the Lord and see how they are doing" (15:36). (b) *For personal reflection. Sharing optional.* Don't pressure anyone to answer this question, but allow those who are willing to do so. If you can, share a personal example where someone expressed concern for your spiritual life and growth.

17. Barnabas was replaced by Silas on Paul's second mission journey. Barnabas, accompanied by his cousin John Mark, went to Cyprus to visit the church there. This break was not permanent. In 1 Corinthians 9:6 Paul holds up Barnabas as a noble example of a missionary supporting himself with his own work. Legend has it that Barnabas was stoned to death in Salamis (a city on Cyprus). As for John Mark himself, he appears in Philemon 24 as a fellow worker with Paul. He is recommended to the church at Colosse (Colossians 4:10), where he is called the "cousin of Barnabas." That Mark was fully reinstated into Paul's favor is shown by the last reference to him, in 2 Timothy 4:11, where Paul desires Mark's companionship in his last days. Silas was eminently qualified to accompany and assist Paul as a missionary, since Silas was a leader in the church and was a prophet (a preacher of God's Word).

18. Encourage participants to share something from their study that they anticipate will be helpful to them.

The Gospel Is Received and Rejected (Paul's Second Mission Journey—Part 1)

Acts 16:1–17:15

Preparing for the Session

Central Focus

The Holy Spirit guided Paul and his missionary companions to take the Gospel to Europe, where it was gladly received by some and passionately rejected by others in Philippi, Thessalonica, and Berea.

Objectives

That participants, led by the Holy Spirit, will

1. understand that some receive the Gospel with a faith that is the gift and work of the Holy Spirit, while others reject the Gospel with an unbelief that is the product of their own sinful human nature;
2. be grateful that the Holy Spirit enabled them to receive and believe the Gospel;
3. courageously stand by the Gospel and tell the Good News to others.

Small-Group Discussion Helps

Day 1 • Acts 16:1–10

1. (a) Paul lists qualities required of pastors, also called elders or overseers (bishops) in the New Testament. The list could be applied to all Christians, but Paul emphasizes that pastors certainly should have all these qualities because of the critical nature of their work. Specific qualities that are similar to "spoken well of" are "above reproach" (v. 2) and "good reputation with outsiders" (v. 7). At Lystra and Iconium it was the members of the church who spoke well of Timothy. But Paul also includes a good reputation among "outsiders." (b) Discuss with your group why it is important that the pastor be spoken well of both inside and outside the church. (c) *For personal reflection. Sharing optional.* Paul refers to Timothy's faith as "sincere" and says that it first lived in his grandmother and then in his mother. Let the class identify people who were involved in the development of their faith, such as parents, grandparents, pastors, teachers, and Sunday school teachers.

2. **Challenge question.** (a) Being circumcised would help Timothy to be accepted as a speaker in synagogues and to enter Jewish homes in order to present the Gospel. (b) Paul wanted to demonstrate that in Christ there is freedom from the requirements of the Jewish ceremonies. At first this might seem inconsistent. He had Timothy circumcised in order to help him preach the Gospel to Jews. He refused to circumcise Titus to demonstrate the freedom in the Gospel. The difference is that if he had complied and circumcised Titus at that time, the Judaizers could use that example to ask all Gentile believers to be circumcised.

3. Luke records that they were kept by the Holy Spirit from preaching the word in Asia (v. 6) and that He wouldn't allow them to enter Bithynia. The Spirit could have done this by visions, by prophecy, or by circumstances such as Paul's health. Asia is directly west of the cluster of the Galatian congregations, and Bithynia is north. Later Paul did go to Asia, where a large congregation developed in Ephesus.

4. God directs our life today through (a) Christ, whom we follow as our Lord and King, (b) through the direction He gives in the Scriptures, (c) through the advice and counsel of Christian friends, and (d) through the answers He gives to our prayers.

Day 2 • Acts 16:11–15

5. Lydia was from Thyatira, which was one of the cities of the seven churches addressed by John in the Book of Revelation (Revelation 1:11; 2:18). Thyatira was known for its dyes, purple or crimson made from a shellfish. Lydia was a businesswoman and was probably wealthy, since she had a home large enough to host Paul's team and for the disciples to use as a meeting place. Lydia was a Gentile, a "worshiper of God," a proselyte who prayed with the Jewish community.

6. There may have been a lack of Jewish men in Philippi because it was a Roman colony, a settlement of Roman citizens. The city was originally known as Krenides, but when Philip II of Macedonia captured it (356 B.C.), he renamed it Philippi after himself. When Emperor Claudius expelled the Jews from Rome (Acts 18:2), the colonies had to follow suit. The pattern in the early church was that when the head of the house came to faith, the rest of the household followed the example. In the story of the jailer the same pattern was followed (v. 33). While only God can create faith, through the power of the Gospel, He can use the example of respected people to open minds and hearts to be receptive to hearing the Gospel.

7. The theme of the Book of Acts is the spread of the Gospel from Jerusalem to Rome. Luke is concerned to show that as the Gospel was spread many people came to faith and were saved. Luke records some specific numbers at first and then keeps saying that many came to faith or that the numbers increased. Verse 14 points out that "the Lord opened her heart to respond." The Gentile Lydia had learned about God and the hope of a Messiah from her contacts with the Jewish people and thus was prepared to hear about the fulfillment of the promise in Jesus of Nazareth. 1 Corinthians 12:3 reminds us that "no one can say, 'Jesus is Lord,' except by the Holy Spirit."

Day 3 • Acts 16:16–34

8. **Challenge question.** (a) The word "troubled" (NIV) is translated in the King James Version as "grieved." The original word means "deeply distressed." Paul, from the first day the spirit yelled at him, was grieved over the condition of the girl who was possessed by an evil spirit and used by her owners for profit. He did not take action at first in order not to stir up trouble. When he did react to the evil spirit, a riot resulted, and he had to leave the city and could no longer preach there. (b) The future is in God's hands, and, while it is not wrong in itself to wonder about what tomorrow will bring, it is wrong to worry and fret about it. Using fortune-telling devices shows an unwillingness to leave it all in God's hands. In fact, such practices not only reveal an unwillingness to leave the future in God's hands but a desire to take the future out of God's hands! God speaks of occult practices (sorcery, fortune-telling, casting spells, consulting the dead, etc.) as detestable and forbids His people to engage in such practices. Instead, God's people are to look to Jesus for help in dealing with both the present and the future.

9. While the Romans used rods, the Jews used whips as a method of punishment or as a way to get an accused to confess. The Jews counted each whip lash and made the limit 40 minus one, or 39. The Romans did not count. The lictors would beat until the officials told them to stop. Paul says that he received the 39 lashes five different times and the rods three times. The beating administered at Philippi was one of those times. We have no record of the others.

10. (a) The jailer had chained Paul and Silas and bound their feet but could not bind their lips. We don't know why the other two members of the team, Timothy and Luke, did not go through the same ordeal as Paul and Silas. Paul and Silas were probably in too much pain to sleep, so singing would help them endure the situation and pass the time. Remembering that the persecution was a sign of their discipleship, blessed by Christ Himself, was no doubt the chief strengthening power that led them to break out in song and prayer. Did they pray for the disciples in Philippi, for the jailer, for the other prisoners, or all of that and more? (b) Often in times of sickness we can be so physically weak that we do not have enough energy to pray and sing. But even in such circumstances Christians can and do express their Christian faith with a quiet and gentle cheerfulness. Encourage participants to speak about the times when the Lord enabled them to persevere under distressing circumstances.

11. The jailer was responsible for the prisoners and could be executed in their place if any of them escaped, as the guards were by Herod when Peter was rescued by the angel (Acts 12:19). When the jailer saw the prison doors open, he assumed the prisoners were gone, even though they were all there. He would rather die quickly by his own hand than endure harsher treatment by his superiors.

12. (a) Jesus came into the world to save sinners (1 Timothy 1:15) and (b) anyone who calls on His name will be saved (Romans 10:13). (c) The "message of the cross" is foolishness to some, but it is the power of God to believers (1 Corinthians 1:18).

Day 4 • Acts 16:35–40

13. Luke does not indicate any reason why Paul and Silas wanted the magistrates to come personally and take them out of prison. The most logical reason is that they wanted to establish their innocence for the future work of the church in Philippi. They did not want a shadow over the church that would allow others to say that their founders and leaders were criminals!

14. Instead of looking for sympathy because of the suffering and humiliation they had endured, Paul and Silas met with the fledgling congregation at Philippi to encourage them. What happened to Paul and Silas might have intimidated or frightened these new Christians. It was important that the apostles reassure them and give them courage.

15. In Philippians 4:16 Paul mentions that the congregation in Philippi sent aid to him when he went on to Thessalonica. In the first chapter of his letter to the Philippians (1:3–11) Paul speaks of his warm feelings toward them, thanking God for every remembrance of them and expressing joy in their partnership in the Gospel. He prays that their love will abound more and more.

Day 5 • Acts 17:1–15

16. Paul and Silas walked the 100 miles, passing through Amphipolis and Apollonia, perhaps stopping overnight at these places. His missionary strategy was to establish centers in important cities, like Thessalonica. Later, in his letter to the congregation there, Paul says that despite the hard beginning (which is recorded here in Acts), they became a "model" for all of Macedonia and Achaia and that the message of the Gospel "rang out" from there throughout the region (1 Thessalonians 1:7–8). Today Thessalonica is known as Thessalonica or Salonika and Berea as Verria.

17. Because of the example of the Bereans in searching the Scripture, the name Berea has been used for some Bible study groups or other organizations in the church. In John 5:39 Jesus told the Jewish leaders that the Scriptures "testify about Me." John concludes his Gospel (John 20:30–31) by telling us that he wrote it so that those who read it might believe and have eternal life. Paul, in writing to Timothy (2 Timothy 3:16–17), says that the "God-breathed" Scripture is useful for teaching, rebuking, correction, training, and equipping Christians for righteous living and good works. Encourage participants to share the way they ended the statement.

18. (a) The Jews who did not believe in "the Christ" or Messiah Paul preached became jealous (v. 5) when they saw their members following Paul. They must have developed strong feelings of bitterness and hatred, for they followed Paul 50 miles to Berea to stir up trouble there against him (v. 13). It seems that they did not have the same antagonism toward Silas and Timothy, who stayed in Berea to carry on the work. Timothy evidently had joined the team after being left to work with Luke in Philippi. Jesus said that the road is narrow and the gate is small that leads to life and only a few find it, while many enter the wide gate on the broad road that leads to destruction (Matthew 7:13–14). (b) The response to the Gospel message has always been that some believe and others reject. After 2,000 years of preaching, only one third of the world population considers themselves Christian. Some have never heard the message, but many have heard and rejected it.

19. Share a favorite verse that impresses you. Many in the class will probably choose 16:31, "Believe in the Lord Jesus, and you will be saved—you and your household."

Getting the Message Straight (Paul's Second Mission Journey—Part 2)

Acts 17:16–18:22

Preparing for the Session

Central Focus

Paul directly confronts Greek paganism in Athens, where he presents the Gospel to people who do not know the true God, and he confronts once again the opposition of Jews in Corinth.

Objectives

That participants, led by the Holy Spirit, will

1. understand better both the difference between the Gospel and all other systems of belief and the points of contact between the Gospel and other systems of belief;
2. desire to prepare themselves for opportunities to present the Gospel to unbelievers;
3. become more effective witnesses of the Gospel;
4. value and utilize the partnership of fellow Christians in the task of presenting the Gospel to the world.

Small-Group Discussion Helps

Day 1 • Acts 17:16–21

1. (a) Paul could not just sit and do nothing while he waited. He had to use his time to share the Gospel, especially since he was distressed over the idols he saw in the city. There were so many idols in Athens that people said, "It is easier to see a god in Athens than a man." These idol worshipers were without Christ, under the influence and power of the devil and demons, and lost for eternity. (b) Encourage the class to discuss evidence of unbelief and being lost from God that they see in the world today and to express their own sensitivity toward those who are lost.

2. (a) The Epicurean philosophy stemmed from Epicurus (341–270 B.C.). Epicureans were almost atheists. They said, "What gods exist are so far removed from people that they are not involved with our lives." Today we hear such comments as "You only go round once" and "Get it while you can." (b) The Stoic philosophy originated with Zeno (332–262 B.C.), who taught at the Stoa (porch) of the public marketplace, and so his teaching was called Stoicism. It was pantheistic, seeing god as something like a soul to the universe. Some of their ideas are found today in aspects of the New Age Movement.

3. Get specific with the group as they respond to how "we" might reach the unchurched in our community. The unchurched do not come to church! Ask such questions as "Where do you talk to an unchurched person?" "When do you talk to such people?" Lots of opportunities to tell the Gospel to unchurched people exist in everyday contacts.

4. When Paul reasoned in the synagogue, he may have used a text from the Scripture readings of the day and presented arguments about how it was fulfilled in Christ. But in the marketplace he had to use a different approach, since the unchurched do not accept the Bible as their source of truth. His approach was more philosophic, as we see in the way he spoke in the meeting of the Areopagus, which will be studied on Day 2. (a) Verse 18: "seems to be advocating foreign gods"; verse 19: "new teaching"; verse 20 "strange ideas." (b) The word *babbler,* before it came to be used for a person as in this text, denoted a bird who skipped about picking up a piece of grain here and there. Paul did digest what he preached! In Galatians 2:19–20 he says he was crucified, he died, and now he is a different person because Christ lives in him. In Philippians 3:8–11 he says everything in life is rubbish except knowing Christ. (c) When Paul came to the bodily resurrection, some of the listeners "sneered" (v. 32). They had had enough. Paul says that Christ crucified was a stumbling block to the Jews and foolishness to the Gentiles (1 Corinthians 1:23). Some might suggest that Paul could have held off speaking about the crucifixion and resurrection of the body until after he talked about love and peace and morality. But to Paul the death and bodily resurrection of Christ were the heart of the message. Without it his message would be distorted, and there would be no power of God (Romans 1:16).

Day 2 • Acts 17:22–31

5. Paul started his missionary work in the marketplace, and because of the interest in his message he was invited to speak to the upper council. Paul began by complimenting the "men of Athens," saying that they were "very religious" (v. 22), a characteristic of which

they were proud. He identified with them by speaking of one of their altars and quoting their poets (v. 28). There were many "unknown god" altars in Athens. Six hundred years before, during a terrible pestilence, a flock of sheep was released from the Areopagus. They were followed, and when they lay down they were sacrificed on the nearest altar. If there was no altar nearby, one was built and a sacrifice made to an "unknown god." Paul quoted from the Cretan poet Epimenides (c. 600 B.C.) and the Cilician poet Aratus (c. 315–240 B.C.).

6. *God*

1. (v. 24a) God made the world and everything in it.
2. (v. 24b) God does not live in temples.
3. (v. 25) God needs nothing from humans.
4. (v. 26a) God made every nation from one man.
5. (v. 26b) God guides history.

People

1. (v. 27) People are to seek, search, and find God.
2. (v. 28) People are His offspring.
3. (v. 30) People are to repent.
4. (v. 31) People will be judged by a man God appointed.

Proof

(v. 31) Proof of it all is that God raised this man from the dead.

7. Though Paul speaks of people seeking God and perhaps reaching out and finding Him (v. 27), phrases with which philosophers would be quite comfortable, Paul also emphasizes that it is actually God who is reaching out to us and finding us. "God did this" and "He is not far from each one of us" (v. 27). Though before they come to faith we might speak to people as if they are looking for God, after people have come to faith they know that actually God came looking for them and found them!

Day 3 • Acts 17:32–18:4

8. While Dionysius was a member of the council, Damaris could not have been because she was a woman. Paul addressed the "Men of Athens." Women were held in low esteem, usually restricted to staying home and caring for their daughters. Damaris may have been a "God-fearing" Gentile in the synagogue or may have heard Paul speak in the marketplace. Perhaps the response to Paul's preaching was so small because these cultured Athenians thought they knew it all and had no need for the Gospel.

9. (a) Paul mentions in 1 Corinthians 6:9–11 the sexually immoral, homosexuals, idolaters, adulterers, thieves, drunkards, slanderers, and swindlers and said, "That is what some of you were" before you were washed, sanctified, justified. (b) We ought not write off anyone when it comes to sharing the Gospel. No matter how we may disapprove and deplore someone's behavior or lifestyle, we can offer God's forgiveness and love to that person. After all, Christ Himself associated with prostitutes and other "low-lifes," not because He approved of their behavior but because He had come to save sinners, even such sinners as these.

10. The word for *tentmaker* is a broad term that could include making sails and ropes for the ships that were near Saul's home in Tarsus. (Tarsus was on the Cydnus River, 10 miles inland from the Mediterranean Sea.) In 1 Corinthians 9:1–15 Paul says that he has a right to expect support but yet he worked (1 Thessalonians 2:9; 2 Thessalonians 3:7–8) so that he would not be a burden to his congregations. Some congregations, such as the Macedonians mentioned in 2 Corinthians 11:9, did send him additional support.

11. (a) There were Jews and/or proselytes in Jerusalem for the Passover on the Day the Holy Spirit was poured out. Some of them were baptized among the 3,000 and returned with the Good News to Pontus. The Jews were expelled from Rome because of the trouble they (or they and the Christians) were causing. Later they were allowed to return. When Paul left Corinth, he took Priscilla and Aquila with him and left them in Ephesus to help carry on his work (Acts 18:18–19). They were well founded in the faith and were able to help the enthusiastic preacher Apollos better understand it (Acts 18:26) (b) Aquila and Priscilla not only provided Paul a place to stay and to work, they also became "fellow workers" with Paul (Romans 16:3–4).

Day 4 • Acts 18:5–11

12. (a) Jesus wept over the city of Jerusalem because He wanted to gather its residents (the Jews), as a hen gathers her chicks, but they "were not willing." (b) **Challenge question**. In Matthew 27:24–25 Pilate washed his hands in front of the people as if to wash the guilt of Jesus' death from his hands. The Jews responded, "Let His blood be on us and on our children." Paul acknowledged that his first responsibility was to witness to the Jews (Romans 1:16), but when they rejected him, he would give his full attention to the Gentiles. Though the Jews had had an opportunity to be saved by believing the Gospel, they had rejected it and so brought the consequences of their rejection upon themselves. (c) When Paul was rejected by the Jews, he went next door to the home of a believing Gentile. There he found the Gospel

enthusiastically received by many. When the Lord closes one door, He often opens a window! Instead of feeling hurt when our efforts are futile in one area, look for the Lord to provide opportunities in another area. Be faithful in sharing the Gospel where and when you can; let the Holy Spirit concern Himself with the results.

13. Paul was dealing with the factions that had developed in the church at Corinth, each group loyal to their perceived leader: Paul, Apollos, Cephas, or Christ (1 Corinthians 1:11–14). Paul declares that he is glad he did not baptize anyone except Crispus and Gaius for, if he had, that might have contributed to the factions. Other members of the missionary team or leaders of the church must have done the baptizing on the mission journeys.

14. The Lord said, "I have many people in this city," and He wanted Paul there to help gather them. Paul stayed another year and a half and evidently reached out from Corinth to the province of Achaia. In 2 Corinthians 1:1 Paul addressed his letter to the church in Corinth and to "all the saints throughout Achaia." In Romans 16:1 he refers to a church in Cenchrea, the seaport town of Corinth.

Day 5 • Acts 18:12–22

15. From ancient records it is known that Gallio was proconsul of the province of Achaia (v. 12) from A.D. 51–52, which dates precisely the time that Paul was there. Sosthenes was either a successor to Crispus, who was baptized (v. 8), or another ruler of the synagogue, since there could be more than one. It hardly seems possible, however, that Crispus could stay in that position after becoming a Christian. Paul included Sosthenes, as a brother, in addressing his first letter to the Corinthian congregation (1 Corinthians 1:1). We cannot be sure why Sosthenes was beaten; perhaps the Jews thought he did not present the case against Paul well enough and he became the way for them to vent their anger and frustration at being rebuffed. Allow participants time to share about times when God protected them.

16. Paul would probably have used the same approach as he did elsewhere, such as before King Agrippa (Acts 26:6–7), namely that Christianity was an extension of Judaism, the fulfillment of the hope of Israel. In his trial before Felix (Acts 24:14–15), Paul said that he worshiped the God of the fathers and believed the Law and prophets. Today many Jews who reject Christianity would not agree that Christianity is a fulfillment of Judaism, although Jews who are Christians proudly make that claim.

17. Paul's vow (v. 18) is not mentioned anywhere else. Some scholars point out that grammatically the vow could have been Aquila's, who is mentioned in the previous sentence. Encourage the class to think of special offerings, special service projects, retreats, pilgrimages, and such.

18. Paul was very conscious that God was in charge of all he did. Encourage the class to discuss how they keep reminding themselves to put God in charge of their own lives.

A Ministry of Miracles (Paul's Third Mission Journey)

Acts 18:23–20:38

Preparing for the Session

Central Focus

Paul's third mission journey included a three-year ministry in Ephesus, where he established the church in that important center of Asia (today's western Turkey). From there he revisited Macedonia and Greece (Achaia) and made his way back to the Holy Land by way of the coast of Asia.

Objectives

That participants, led by the Holy Spirit, will

1. be more aware of the difference between the Gospel and the beliefs and values frequently found in the world about us;
2. desire to avoid all forms of superstition and occult practices;
3. be willing to teach and guide fellow Christians in a way that will bring their understanding and beliefs more in line with the Gospel;
4. value Christian fellowship.

Small-Group Discussion Helps

Day 1 • Acts 18:23–19:7

1. (a) *The Scriptures*: Apollos had a thorough knowledge of the Scripture (v. 24) and proved from Scripture that Jesus was the Christ (v. 28). (b) *Jesus:* Apollos had been instructed in the "way of the Lord" and taught about Jesus accurately (v. 25). (c) *Style of teaching and preaching:* Apollos spoke with great fervor (v. 25). He glowed with enthusiasm and zeal. Apollos spoke boldly (v. 26) and vigorously refuted the Jews (v. 28).

2. Explain that John's baptism was not invalid, just obsolete. John's baptism was one of repentance, baptizing people who confessed and repented of their sins. It was a mark of repentance in anticipation and preparation for the One who was to come. Jesus' Baptism is based on the accomplished work of the atonement through His death and resurrection and is done in the name of the Triune God—Father, Son, and Holy Spirit.

3. (a) Encourage participants to speak about couples they have known who have impressed them by their teamwork in serving God. Participants may think first about pastors and their wives, but suggest also that they think of other Christian couples who have served the Lord together. (b) Let participants share in their own words what 2 Timothy 3:16–17 has to say.

Day 2 • Acts 19:8–22

4. While Christians are not to be manipulative in attempting to persuade others of the truth of the Gospel, the urgency of the message of salvation through Christ calls for our best efforts in presenting this Good News. In 2 Corinthians 5:20 Paul says, "we *implore* you on Christ's behalf: Be reconciled to God."

5. Paul explains in Romans 14:17 that the kingdom of God is not a material reality (not "eating and drinking") but a spiritual reality ("righteousness, peace and joy in the Holy Spirit"). Jesus told Pilate, "My kingdom is not of this world" (John 18:36). This so-called "Kingdom of Grace" is the rule of God in the hearts of all who believe in Christ.

6. It is uncertain how the term "the Way" came to be used to describe the Christians. It may have roots in the words of Jesus, "I am the way ..." (John 14:6). Its first appearance in Acts is at 9:2, where Paul sets out for Damascus searching for anyone who belongs to the Way in order to arrest them. It is used twice by the Ephesians in Acts 19:9, 23. Paul himself used it twice: Acts 22:4, 24:14. The last time it is used is to tell us that Felix was well acquainted with "the Way" (Acts 24:22). Let participants share ideas of what the term conveys: a way of life, a way of thinking, the right teaching, the things Jesus taught, and so on.

7. (a) **Challenge question.** While the seven sons of Sceva invoked the name of Jesus as they tried to drive demons out of people, it is clear that they themselves did not have personal faith in Jesus. They simply used His name as an incantation. Saying the name of Jesus in itself accomplishes nothing; calling upon Jesus in faith is what is important. (b) Jesus Himself prayed (and still prays) for us, that we might be protected from the power of the devil. The fact that Jesus Himself intercedes on our behalf will certainly give us confidence as we face the devil and the evil he brings about in this world. Because of Jesus, our own prayers are also heard by God. (c) Verses 17–20 describe these things: (1) people were seized with fear; (2) the name of Jesus was

held in high honor; (3) many openly confessed evil deeds; (4) sorcery scrolls were burned; (5) God's Word spread and grew in power.

8. Paul preached in the synagogue for three months, and verse 10 adds that he taught in the lecture hall of Tyrannus for two years. All the "Jews and Greeks who lived in the province of Asia heard the word of the Lord" (v. 10) and "the word of the Lord spread widely and grew in power" (v. 20). These were good reasons to stay for three years! Ephesus was the capital of the province of Asia, a city of a quarter million people known for its commerce. It was the market of Asia. Travelers from Ephesus went to all parts of Asia, and some of them helped to spread the Gospel.

Day 3 • Acts 19:23–41

9. Demetrius and the craftsmen of related trades were making a good living with the shrines of Artemis, and they didn't want any religious sect to cut into their business. Like a union organizer, he sought to rally the support of all the workers. He charged that the trade would lose its good name, the temple would be discredited, and that the goddess Artemis would be "robbed of her divine majesty" (v. 27). The charges had some truth to them but were gross exaggerations.

10. *Background:* Diana, the Roman goddess of the moon, was a daughter of Jupiter and the twin sister of Apollo. She was represented as a virgin huntress. When the Greek worship penetrated Italy, the Italians identified Diana with the Greek goddess Artemis. Former Bible translations all used *Diana* in these verses while the most recent ones use *Artemis*. The original image of Artemis was said to have fallen from heaven. It, or the idea for it, may have come from a meteorite. She was the goddess of the sexual instinct. For the Ephesians she, with her many breasts, was the great Asiatic nursing mother of gods, men, animals, and plants.

Certainly sexual sins are connected with many other sins in our world also, including drug and alcohol abuse, abortions, thievery, and murders. Group members may think of many other examples. Legal business interests through the advertising of many kinds of useful products and the sale of harmful products may encourage such sins as envy and covetousness, drunkenness, the abuse of one's own health and of the health of others, and sexual sins of many kinds. Illegal business interests such as prostitution and drug trafficking certainly cause much misery and suffering not only to their customers but to many others.

11. (a) Riots and mob violence no doubt have many causes, such as greed, fears, racial prejudice, envy, and ignorance. Some people, no doubt, simply get caught up in the excitement of such events. (b) Satan, and those who act under his influence, delights in stirring up such violence, particularly when he can do harm to the cause of the Gospel or to Christians. Encourage participants to share their thoughts.

Day 4 • Acts 20:1–12

12. Paul spoke "many words of encouragement" (20:2) to the churches he visited, as was his usual practice. He would give them further instruction about faith in Christ and urge them to continue to walk in the truth of the Gospel.

13. The list of seven included some men who were fellow workers with Paul and others who were primarily delegates elected by their congregations to represent them and help deliver the offering to the Jerusalem church. (a) *How:* Paul tells the congregation in Corinth that they should set aside some money every time they worship together on the first day of the week, Sunday. The amount was to be "in keeping with his income" or, as we say today, proportionate giving. Then, when Paul arrived, the money would be ready and there would be no need for an emergency collection. (b) *Why:* The collection was to be for the poor in the church in Jerusalem. The Gentiles had shared in the Jews' spiritual blessings of the Messiah, and now they would share their material blessings with the Jews.

14. Encourage participants to point out connections they see between Jesus' resurrection and their Sunday worship. Some might point out that the service strikes a note of celebration and joy, or that the sermon and various parts of the worship proclaim the Gospel of forgiveness and grace through Jesus, which the resurrection guarantees. Some might refer to Holy Baptism, which is the resurrection of the new self with Christ. Some might refer to lighted candles, which represent the presence of the risen Christ among us. Probably you will come up with a long list of such connections.

15. Paul threw himself on Eutychus and put his arms around him. Peter (Acts 9:40) merely prayed for Dorcas (*Tabitha* in Aramaic), and she was restored to life. Elijah (1 Kings 17:19–23) did both: he prayed and stretched his body on the lad. In any case, there is only one way to account for these miraculous restorations—the power of God that responded to the prayers of Paul, Peter, and Elijah.

Day 5 • Acts 20:13–38

16. **Challenge question**. Paul's ship did not stop at Ephesus but went to Miletus, 30 miles away. He was in a hurry to get to Jerusalem by Pentecost, so instead of

walking to Ephesus, he asked the elders to come to him. (a) Paul served the Lord with great humility and tears (v. 19). Paul was not ashamed of his tears. He cried at the final farewell when he boarded his ship (v. 37). He speaks about many "tears" when he warned the Philippians (Philippians 3:18) and tells the Corinthians that he wrote to them with "great distress and anguish of heart and with many tears" (2 Corinthians 2:4). (b) Paul preached what would be helpful to God's people (v. 20)—repentance and faith (v. 21), the Gospel of God's grace (v. 24), the kingdom (v. 25), and the "whole will of God" (v. 27). (c) Paul taught publicly and from house to house (v. 20). (d) Paul declared to Jews and Greeks (v. 21). (e) Paul warned them day and night with tears (v. 31). (f) Paul supplied his own needs (vv. 33–34). We know that Paul also worked in Corinth (18:3) and in Thessalonica (1 Thessalonians 2:9) to support himself.

17. Paul shares with us that life on earth with all of its pleasures and riches meant nothing to him. The only thing that counted was to finish the race and complete the task God had given him, to testify to the Gospel of God's grace. Other translations use different words for "race" and "task." Paul says in the next chapter that he was ready to be bound and die if necessary when he went to Jerusalem (Acts 21:13).

18. (a) A pastor is to "keep watch" (v. 28) over what is entrusted to him by Jesus, the Shepherd and Overseer (1 Peter 2:25): the flock He purchased with His own blood. But in order to keep watch over the flock he must first keep watch over himself lest he be led astray or destroyed by the same enemies that attack the flock. (b) The pastor's responsibility is to love the flock as Jesus, the Good Shepherd, did when He laid down His life for it (John 10:11). Paul wanted to protect his flock from those false teachers who would come in among them and destroy their faith by distorting the Gospel.

19. At this time Paul thought this would be his last chance to say anything to these pastors. So he tells them to be on guard against the savage wolves from outside and the false teachers inside the church, and he committed them to God and the Word of His grace. Paul knelt down with all of them and prayed on shore. They wept, embraced, and kissed good-bye, and they accompanied him to the ship.

Defending the Ministry—Part 1 (Arrest in Jerusalem)

Acts 21–23

Preparing for the Session

Central Focus

Despite warnings that he would be arrested there, Paul proceeded to Jerusalem. There, as predicted, Paul was falsely accused, became the focus of a riot, and was arrested. He testified before his countrymen and Roman officials and was transferred to Caesarea for his own protection.

Objectives

That participants, led by the Holy Spirit, will

1. understand more clearly that God was directing the course of Paul's apostolic ministry;
2. feel confident that God is guiding the course of their own lives as they faithfully follow the Lord's Word;
3. courageously witness to others about the Lord's grace, guidance, and blessing in their own lives.

Small-Group Discussion Helps

Day 1 • Acts 21:1–19

1. (a) Paul said that he was going to Jerusalem "compelled" by the Holy Spirit (Acts 20:22). (b) The Spirit had also revealed to Paul that he would have prison and hardship in Jerusalem (20:23). (c) The disciples in Tyre were told "through the Spirit" what would happen to Paul; this led them to urge him not to go (21:4). (d) Agabus, a prophet from Judea, warned that Paul would be bound by the Jews and turned over to the Gentiles (21:11). The Spirit showed Paul what would happen to him in Jerusalem and later revealed to Paul that God was sending him to Rome to bear testimony for Jesus there (23:11).

2. Philip was chosen as one of the seven deacons (Acts 6:5) and preached with "miraculous signs" in Samaria (8:4–8). The Spirit led him to teach the Gospel to the Ethiopian on the Gaza road and then sent him to Caesarea, the important capital of Judea, where Paul met him. Philip had left Jerusalem with the lay people who were scattered because of the persecutions led by Saul (Acts 8:1, 4–5).

3.(a) "For the name of the Lord Jesus" (v. 13) centers in the message of the Gospel of God's grace (20:24). (b) The Lord's will, which Paul was so willing to submit to, is that the Good News (the Gospel) of God's love for sinners be communicated to people so that sinners may be brought to faith in Christ.

4. Paul certainly fostered the warm, loving spirit shown to him by James and the elders of Jerusalem by giving them a full, detailed report of all of his missionary activities.

Day 2 • Acts 21:20–40

5. (a) Paul always spoke of "what *God had done* among the Gentiles through his ministry" (v. 19). Similar phrases are found in Acts 15:4 "everything *God* had done through them"; 15:7—"*God* made a choice among you that the Gentiles might hear from my lips the message of the gospel and believe"; 15:8—"He [God] accepted them by giving the Holy Spirit to them"; 15:12—"the miraculous signs and wonders *God* had done among the Gentiles through them." (b) We certainly want to give God credit when He brings people to faith through us or through others, for He has done it. We can praise God for His grace when we refer to these conversions, and we can thank Him in our prayers.

6. The report they heard was that Paul was teaching *the Jews* who lived among the Gentiles scattered around the world that they should "turn away from Moses," "not ... circumcise their children," and not "live according to our customs" (v. 21). Paul did teach that both Jew and Gentile are justified by faith in Jesus Christ and not by keeping the Law. There was nothing wrong with keeping the Law as long as it was voluntary and no merit was placed on its observance (Galatians 2:15–16). Paul himself chose to demonstrate that freedom by refusing to circumcise Titus, who was a Greek (Galatians 2:3–5).

7. Responses will vary—and, to be sure, a lot of factors enter in: for example, whether the nonkneeling member has a physical problem that makes kneeling difficult, the context of the criticism, and the attitude behind the criticism. Hopefully, the discussion will conclude that posture in prayer or any other religious custom does not by itself determine whether one is or is not a Christian. We would lovingly want to maintain

that any "custom" that we adduce as a proof or non-proof of our Christianity is contrary to the only foundation—faith in Christ for the forgiveness of sin. On the one hand, when this truth of the Gospel is at stake, a Christian must stand loving but firm in what he or she says and does. On the other hand, if the Gospel is not compromised, we are called to be as loving and accommodating as the Spirit gives us power, to not offend and to help our weak brothers and sisters grow in their understanding of the Gospel. Thus, one might well be led to say, in the hypothetical example, "Yes, I'll be glad to kneel for prayer here at St. Matthew. It's certainly a custom I can learn to appreciate, even though my faith and yours are not dependent on it. Isn't it great that we can praise God for His forgiveness in Jesus?"

8. The vow was probably a temporary Nazirite vow (Numbers 6:2–20). It was an act of piety to pay the cost of the sacrifices, in this case eight pigeons and four lambs, for those who were poor. Paul was willing to do anything to keep from hindering the spread of the Gospel. He told the Corinthians that he was free but willingly made himself a slave to all, becoming as much like each group as possible (Jews, those under the Law, those not having the Law, the weak) in order to win some of them (1 Corinthians 9:19–23).

9. (a) The size and intensity of the mob is expressed in words like "whole city," "dragged him," "trying to kill him," "beating Paul." (b) A Roman legion consisted of 6,000 soldiers, with each cohort of 1,000 men commanded by a "chiliarch" or tribune, each 100 men by a centurion. The commander, Claudius Lysias, was a chiliarch. He brought "some officers and soldiers" (v. 32), perhaps 200, to stop the riot. Roman justice forbade lynching and insisted on a fair trial for everyone.

Day 3 • Acts 22:1–21

10. Paul could have tried to argue that he did not bring Trophimus into the temple, that he did not teach Jews to give up the laws of Moses. But instead he gave his personal testimony, a true story with which they could not argue. (a) Paul had spoken Greek to the Roman commander, who was now surprised to hear Paul speak in Aramaic. If Paul had spoken in Hebrew it would have been more difficult for the people to understand since they normally did not speak in that formal language. It is good to try to identify with the people to whom we witness, but there are limits as to how far we adopt their slang. For instance, we don't have to curse when we talk to a person who always curses. (b) In Philippians 3:5–6 he says that he was circumcised, of the tribe of Benjamin, and a Pharisee. (c) Paul had studied under Gamaliel, a respected and widely known rabbi. Someone who had studied under such a prominent teacher would be treated more considerately by Jews.

11. The terms that indicate that God's initiative made Paul an apostle are "assigned to do" (v. 10), "chosen" (v. 14), and "send you" (v. 21).

12. **Challenge question.** (a) The term "Righteous One" recalls the reference in Isaiah 53:11 to "My Righteous Servant." Peter called Jesus the "Holy and Righteous One" (3:14). Stephen referred to "the Righteous One." Responses from the class about the meaning may include that Jesus is "right," holy, perfect, God. (b) When Judas was replaced (Acts 1:22–22), one of the requirements for the candidates was that they had seen the risen Lord. Paul was proud of the fact that he had seen Jesus, both at his conversion and then later in a vision in Jerusalem (v. 17). Paul was called to be an apostle to the Gentiles, although one "abnormally born," that is, one whose calling to become an apostle came later than the calls of the Twelve (1 Corinthians 9:1; 15:8).

13. In his sermon on Pentecost day, Peter admonishes his hearers to be baptized "for the forgiveness of … sins" (Acts 2:38). Paul speaks to the Ephesians about "cleansing her [the church] by the washing with water through the word" (Ephesians 5:26). Martin Luther referred to the role of water in Baptism in this way: "Certainly not just water, but the word of God in and with the water does these things, along with the faith which trusts this word of God in the water" (*Luther's Small Catechism with Explanation*, St. Louis: Concordia Publishing House, 1991, p. 22).

Day 4 • Acts 22:22–23:11

14. Paul's mention that he was sent by God to the Gentiles (v. 21) triggered the reoccurrence of the violence aroused by the original charges against Paul by the Asian Jews (21:27–28), which were that Paul taught against the Jewish people, their law, and the temple, and that he had brought a Greek into the temple. To put the Gentiles on a par with them was an insult to their national religion and pride.

15. The commander originally thought Paul was an Egyptian who had led a revolt (21:38) and still suspected he might be. He may not have understood what Paul said when he was speaking in Aramaic to the crowd. Flogging was the way to find out the truth (vv. 24, 29). Jesus' flogging was different in that it was meant to make Him suffer and stir up pity from His accusers (John 19:1–5). Allow the class to discuss such freedoms as listed in the U.S. Bill of Rights or the Canadian Constitution, including the privilege of voting, free speech, worship, holding office, protection, and owning prop-

erty. Emphasize that these rights allow us to proclaim the Gospel freely and to share it openly with our neighbors.

16. (a) Paul had not been condemned and had not done anything to deserve the blow. The high priest was breaking Jewish law with this order. This high priest Ananias is not the Annas of Jesus' day, but was known for his cruelty and hardness. (b) In verse 5 Paul quoted Exodus. Whitewashed wall or tomb means that the exterior is beautiful but it covers evil or dead bones. To touch a tomb made an Israelite unclean, so Israelites whitewashed their tombs in order to prevent touching them by mistake. "Whitewashed" was another way of saying, "You are a *hypocrite.*" A hypocrite covers up the real person or feelings by a superficial front.

17. Paul may have realized that it was hopeless to get a fair hearing with the Sanhedrin and so brought up the resurrection in order to create dissension and confusion.

Day 5 • Acts 23:12–35

18. (a) Claudius Lysias could have released Paul but he was probably afraid of another riot. Felix kept Paul in prison for the two years he remained in Caesarea (Acts 24:27) for political reasons, to please the Jews. He also might have been expecting a bribe. In the hands of the Sanhedrin Paul could have been killed, as Stephen was. Paul appears to have received the best treatment at the hands of Claudius Lysias. (b) God had told Paul that he was going to preach the Gospel in Rome (Acts 23:11). Through all the trials Paul believed that God would protect him and somehow lead him to Rome. (c) Encourage group members to describe periods in their own lives when God seemed to have been arranging things so they might have an opportunity to witness concerning Jesus.

19. Encourage group members to share their answers. It may help to get the discussion started if you share first.

Defending the Ministry—Part 2 (Imprisonment in Caesarea)

Acts 24–26

Preparing for the Session

Central Focus

Paul is tried before two Roman governors, Felix and Festus, and has a hearing before a king, Agrippa II. Paul appeals to Caesar's judgment of his case and is to be transferred to Rome. At his trials and hearing, Paul witnesses to his faith in Jesus as the Savior and even urges his judges to join him in this faith!

Objectives

That participants, led by the Holy Spirit, will

1. be aware of how Paul used every opportunity to proclaim the Gospel to others;
2. desire to share the Gospel with others at every available opportunity;
3. be more skillful in recognizing and more ready to seize opportunities to speak the Gospel.

Small-Group Discussion Helps

Day 1 • Acts 24:1–21

1. It took only five days (v. 1) for Ananias to get a delegation together, hire a lawyer, and get to Felix's court 60 miles away. The charges against Paul are (a) He is a troublemaker (v. 5); (b) He stirs up riots among Jews all over the world (v. 5); (c) He is a ringleader of the Nazarene sect (v. 5); and (d) He tried to desecrate the temple (v. 6).

2. Paul responded to each of the charges in his own way, not with arguments but in direct, plain statements. (a and b) Paul answered the first two charges (that he was a troublemaker and caused riots) together by dismissing them as lies. He used words like "did not find me arguing" (v. 12) and "cannot prove to you the charges" (v. 13). He was confident that if they brought witnesses the governor would find out the truth. (c) As to being a ringleader of the Nazarene sect, Paul confessed that he was a follower of "the Way" (v. 14), which they called a sect. But belonging to a sect was no crime; even the Sadducees and Pharisees were called sects ("party" in some translations; 5:17; 26:5). Paul's defense was that he was a good Jew! He agreed with the Law and prophets (v. 14) and believed in the resurrection. (d) Against the charge of trying to desecrate the temple, Paul said that he had brought an offering, was ceremonially clean in the temple, brought no crowd, and caused no disturbance. He assumed Felix would believe him or call witnesses, if necessary.

3. Paul insisted that he believed in the same hope as the Jews who were accusing him—the hope of a resurrection of both the "righteous and the wicked" (v. 15). (a) Job declared his faith that his Redeemer lives and would one day stand upon the earth and that Job himself, even after his death, would look upon God with his own eyes. (b) In the song of faith and praise recorded in Isaiah 26, the conviction is expressed that the dead would live and that their bodies would rise from the dust of the earth. (c) The prophet Daniel said that "multitudes who sleep in the dust of the earth will awake: some to everlasting life, others to shame and everlasting contempt" (Daniel 12:2). (d) And Martha assumed her brother Lazarus would rise again (John 11:24).

Day 2 • Acts 24:22–25:12

4. Since Luke records the charges against Paul and his defense in such detail, he probably would have recorded any further proceedings prior to the adjournment. (a) Felix probably thought that Paul or his friends had money since they brought the offering to Jerusalem (Acts 24:17), so he hoped for a bribe (v. 26), a common practice. (b) This was a delicate political situation and Felix sought to win the favor of the Jews (v. 27, Acts 25:9). Felix was later recalled to Rome to answer for injustices he was accused of in his dealings with the Jews and the Syrians.

5. (a) Felix talked to Paul frequently (v. 26) and at least once with his third wife, Drusilla (daughter of Herod Agrippa I). Paul spoke about faith in Jesus. Luke notes that Felix "listened" (v. 24). Paul also talked about righteousness, self-control, and the judgment to come (v. 25). The judgment to come may have caused Felix to think about his own life and so become afraid. (b) Encourage participants to say why they think the idea of a coming judgment does or does not cause our contemporaries to be apprehensive. (c) By putting off a consideration of their own sin and their need for forgiveness and life through faith in Christ, many today choose death for themselves.

6. Christianity would get a lot of publicity in a trial before Caesar, and many people in high places would hear the message. This was one way for Paul to get to Rome. If he were acquitted before Caesar, Christianity would have some official recognition.

Day 3 • Acts 25:13–27

7. Bernice at age 13 married her uncle, Herod of Calcis, and when he died, lived with Agrippa II. To silence rumors of incest she married Polemon, king of Cilicia, but soon returned to live with Agrippa. Later she became the mistress of emperor Vespasian's son, Titus. (a) The father of Agrippa II was Herod Agrippa I, who had James beheaded and—seeing how this pleased some of the Jews—also put Peter in prison (Acts 12:1–3). He was a grandson of Herod the Great. (b) Herod Antipas had John the Baptist beheaded, primarily to please his wife and her daughter, Salome, who tricked him (Matthew 14:3–12). (c) Herod the Great had the baby boys two years old and under killed in Bethlehem in his effort to exterminate the baby Jesus (Matthew 2:13–16). (d) Agrippa may have wanted to see Paul because he heard that he was preaching about Jesus and, because of his family's involvement with Jesus, he was concerned.

8. (a) Luke described the charges that were presented to Festus as "many serious charges against [Paul], which they could not prove" (v. 7). These were the same as the original charges, and Paul's defense was the same (Acts 24:5–16). Festus referred to the resurrection of Jesus as the matter of "a dead man named Jesus who Paul claimed was alive" (v. 19). (b) It is clear that Festus did not come close to taking Paul's claims about Jesus seriously. He refers to Jesus as "a dead man ... who Paul claimed was alive." Festus no doubt joined other worldly Gentiles in dismissing the claims of Christianity as foolishness.

Day 4 • Acts 26:1–23

9. By identifying himself as a Jew, Paul is suggesting that the charges are out of place. (a) *Hope* means to look forward to what one doesn't have now. Today we would include our own resurrection and eternal life in our hope (Titus 1:2). That future hope is built on the present hope that God has forgiven our sins for Jesus' sake and that He accepts us into His kingdom already now and claims us as His own people. We hold on to this hope with a feeling of certainty because we have God's own promises to back it up. (b) In verse 22 Paul uses the phrase "prophets and Moses," while Luke, in his Gospel, uses the phrases "beginning with Moses and all the Prophets, ... in all the Scriptures" (Luke 24:27) and "everything must be fulfilled that is written about Me in the Law of Moses, the Prophets and the Psalms" (Luke 24:44). (c) Jesus said in Luke 24:47 that repentance must be preached "to all nations, beginning at Jerusalem." In Acts 1:8 He told His disciples that they would be His witnesses in Jerusalem, Judea, Samaria, and to the "ends of the earth."

10. (a) Before the Sanhedrin Paul made a point of saying that he was "a Pharisee, the son of a Pharisee" (Acts 23:6). A number of times in his epistles he calls himself a Pharisee (e.g., Philippians 3:5–6). As such, he had been zealous, but for the wrong cause. Jesus warns against a zealousness that upholds not God's truth but human traditions. Allow participants to speak about causes for which they are or have been zealous. (b) Let participants also suggest causes they do or have opposed, such as false teaching, pornography, gambling, abortion, or causes that they fight for, such as the election of honest leaders, good education in their community schools, or projects that benefit their community. (c) Encourage participants to speak of how they consider themselves to be commissioned as a servant or witness of Jesus.

11. (a) What wonderful blessings come to people through the Gospel! Among these blessings are having our eyes opened so that we can see and understand the truths of God's Word, be rescued from Satan's tyranny of darkness, and be brought into God's gracious and loving rule. We are removed from the power of Satan and live instead in God's power. In God's wonderful kingdom all of our sins are forgiven, and we live side by side with the holy people of God. (b) "Repent and turn to God and prove their repentance by their deeds" (v. 20). Paul describes his ministry at Ephesus as such, "I have declared to both Jews and Greeks that they must turn to God in repentance and have faith in our Lord Jesus" (Acts 20:21). (c) Some in the class may suggest that we must start by pointing out sin; others might suggest starting with what people already believe or with some problem or hurt in their lives.

Day 5 • Acts 26:24–32

12. Festus had turned the meeting over to Agrippa, who had opened the meeting by giving Paul permission to speak (Acts 26:1). It was still Festus's palace and Paul was still his prisoner, but it was not proper for Festus to suddenly interrupt an "examination" that his guest Agrippa was conducting. There is no way of knowing what Festus was thinking. Allow participants to react to the three suggestions or to voice suggestions of their own.

13. (a) Agrippa's answer reveals his comprehension of both Judaism and Christianity. He used the word *Chris-*

tian, which was coined in Syrian Antioch as a term of mockery (Acts 11:26). Paul knew that Agrippa was more attuned to the prophecies and the Jewish hope than Festus was and hoped that he would confess his faith in the prophets. If Agrippa had said he believed the prophets, then Paul could ask him to believe in Jesus because He fulfilled the prophecies about the resurrection. (b) It is always proper to ask whether a person believes the Gospel we have presented. It is not proper to manipulate people or put pressure on them to answer the way we want them to answer.

14. **Challenge question.** Paul prayed for all who heard him, which meant the "high ranking officers and the leading men of the city" (25:23), as well as the royal courts of Festus and Agrippa. (a) To become what Paul was meant to be a follower of Jesus. (b) In Romans 10:1 Paul said that his "heart's desire and prayer" was that his people, the Jews, might be saved.

The Castastrophic Voyage to Rome

Acts 27

Preparing for the Session

Central Focus

The sea voyage that took Paul to Rome began late in the sailing season, was delayed by contrary winds, and included a terrifying interruption when the ship was wrecked after a violent storm. But God rescued all on the ship for the sake of Paul, His apostle.

Objectives

That participants, led by the Holy Spirit, will

1. understand how the Lord preserved the lives of Paul and his traveling companions for the sake of Paul's Gospel ministry, which was to be continued in Rome;
2. grow more confident of the Lord's direction and protection as they carry out their own service to the Lord;
3. show greater courage in times of crisis on account of this confidence resulting from faith;
4. thank and praise God for His protection and guidance.

Small-Group Discussion Helps

Day 1 • Acts 27:1–8

1. The name "Imperial Regiment" (some translations: "Augustan Cohort") suggests that this centurion might have been from a special corps of troops whose task it was to deliver prisoners and serve as a courier between Rome and the provinces. The other prisoners may have been criminals being taken to Rome for use in the games in the arena with wild animals and gladiators. Julius appears to have been a kind and considerate man, sensitive and a good judge of character. He recognized Paul as an innocent, principled person and respected Paul's opinions. He was courageous and saved Paul's life, even though this meant taking a great personal risk since Julius would have been held personally responsible if any of the prisoners had escaped while fleeing the sinking ship at Malta.

2. It hardly seems likely that Julius would allow Paul to have traveling companions unless they were there for a purpose. Aristarchus may have consented to be considered a slave in order to go with Paul. We know Luke is along because of the use of "we" and "us" in the account. (a) We know that Aristarchus was in Ephesus as Paul's traveling companion from Macedonia (Acts 19:29), (b) that he was from Thessalonica and served as a delegate to deliver the offering (Acts 20:4), and (c) that he was with Paul later in Rome (Colossians 4:10).

3. Paul had been a prisoner in Caesarea for two years. Not being able to work, he had to depend on his friends for his personal needs, such as decent clothing and writing supplies. He needed to be supplied for the trip to Rome. He may also have had to pay the fare for his companions, Luke and Aristarchus. Since these friends were Christians, Paul would have also enjoyed fellowship and mutual strengthening among them.

4. Not all the cities on the trip are mentioned in the text; many fall under the reference to "ports along the coast of the province of Asia" (v. 2). Most Bible maps of the journey indicate some of them, such as Antioch and Tarsus. The ones that are mentioned are Sidon, Myra, Cnidus, Fair Havens, and Lasea. (a) Verse 6—This ship from Egypt was going to Italy. (b) Verse 38—Its cargo was grain, which in the storm was thrown overboard. (c) Verse 37—It was large enough to hold 276 people, counting the prisoners, the soldiers who guarded them, and the crew.

Day 2 • Acts 27:9–20

5. Some people think that God gave Paul some special revelation so that he knew there was danger ahead, although there is no indication of that. Luke records that later an angel appeared to Paul (v. 23), so it seems he would have recorded any visions at this time also. Paul may have been able to "see" (v. 10) on the basis of his experience, having been shipwrecked three times and adrift a day and night (2 Corinthians 11:25).

6. The sailors pulled in the lifeboat (v. 16) that was being towed behind the ship. They tied the ship together with ropes and threw out an anchor to help slow it down (v. 17). They threw cargo overboard, perhaps cargo lashed on the deck (v. 18). They threw the "ship's tackle" overboard (v. 19). This may have been spars, planks, masts, and other items used to drag behind to slow the ship. The storm continued many days and, since they saw no sun or stars, they didn't know where they were and gave up hope of being saved (v. 20).

Day 3 • Acts 27:21–29

7. The account does not mention Paul after his warning in verse 10 until he said, "You should have taken my advice" (v. 21). (a) Let the class respond in various ways, from comments like "He was right!" to "He should have kept his mouth shut!" (b) Paul was not one to boast or show off. He probably wanted to prepare the people for what he was going to say and make them willing to listen to him now. (c) Paul foresaw that the ship would run aground on some island. This would enable those on the ship to save their lives by swimming ashore or floating ashore by holding on to debris from the disintegrating ship.

8. God had promised Paul that he would "testify in Rome" (Acts 23:11) and the way he would get there was to be tried before Caesar (v. 24). The angel reminded Paul of all that. God intended to keep His promise.

9. (a) The Lord sometimes chooses not to rescue us from times of stress but to strengthen us through them by building up perseverance, character, hope, and other Christian virtues. Our faith in the Lord is increased as we learn by experience that we can trust Him. (b) Encourage participants to share their own experiences by which they grew by meeting challenges with faith or received some other blessing

10. The trained ear of the sailors could hear the different sounds in the air, the breakers, and the surf, which told them they were near land. This meant they were in danger of being smashed on rocks. They didn't know where they were. (a) It seems that the "sailors" (v. 27) were the ones who did the praying. There may have been some Jews among them. They may have heard Paul's confession, "the God whose I am and whom I serve" (v. 23) and anything else Paul may have said in witnessing during the trip. Many of them probably prayed to heathen gods. (b) Most people tend to pray more in time of need. We should pray at such times, since God encourages us to pray in the "day of trouble" (Psalm 50:15) and promises to hear us and deliver us. But we miss out on many blessings and deprive ourselves of much strength and joy if we pray only at such times. Paul urges us to pray continually (1 Thessalonians 5:17).

Day 4 • Acts 27:30–38

11. (a) After Paul urged all of them to take some food, he set the example and ate in front of them all. But before he ate, he gave thanks to God. Most others on board were probably pagans who never prayed before they ate. His prayer indicated his trust in God and his authority to say that no one would be harmed. His eating likewise indicated that he trusted God and was not too tense to eat. (b) Before Jesus fed the 5,000 with the five loaves and two fish, He looked up to heaven and gave thanks (Luke 9:16). When He sat down to eat with the Emmaus disciples, He also gave thanks (Luke 24:30). Praying before meals gives us an opportunity to acknowledge God as the Giver of food and all we need, to thank Him, to ask His blessing upon our food, and to remember to share with those who have less than we. (c) **Challenge question.** To be "consecrated by the word of God and prayer" means that God is acknowledged as the Creator and Giver and that His creation is dedicated to the purpose for which He made it and to His glory (1 Timothy 4:4–5). (d) When we bow our heads and pray before a meal in a public place, such as at a restaurant, we provide a witness to those around us. Of course we must be careful that we are not just attempting to impress people with our piety. Jesus condemned hypocrisy and the showing off of religiosity so that people might praise us for it.

12. Jesus used the expression that the hairs of our heads "are all numbered" (Luke 12:7), which indicates that we are important to God and that He will take care of us. What a comfort to know this, especially in times when we are afraid!

13. Encourage the group to share incidents in their lives that helped them evaluate their priorities and what is important in life.

Day 5 • Acts 27:39–44

14. Roman military law exacted the punishment that a prisoner deserved from the soldier or soldiers who were responsible for his escape. Sometimes they put the guards to death, as Herod did when the angel took Peter out of prison (Acts 12:18–19). If the prisoners were allowed to go to shore on their own, they could easily have escaped.

15. It must have been a motley crew, 276 people swimming or holding on to planks and pieces of the ship, but they all made it to shore (vv. 43–44). Let the group share experiences of special rescues by God and what they did to express their appreciation.

16. (a) Luke was an eyewitness. He must also have had a good knowledge of sailing (v. 2). (b) God used the knowledge of Luke and guided his writing. Paul says that the Scriptures are "God-breathed" (2 Timothy 3:16), in other words, all Scripture was inspired by God. Peter says that men spoke as they were "carried along by the Holy Spirit" (2 Peter 1:21)—it was the Holy Spirit who moved God's prophets to speak and write His Word.

17. Some of the class might suggest the promise and protection of God or perhaps the leadership of Paul.

The Gospel Comes to Rome

Acts 28

Preparing for the Session

Central Focus

After wintering on Malta (where Paul demonstrated the power of Jesus by healing many sick people), Paul was taken on to Rome, where he was welcomed by Christians already there and proclaimed the Gospel to Rome's Jewish leaders.

Objectives

That participants, led by the Holy Spirit, will

1. understand better how and why the Holy Spirit gave powerful testimony to the truth of the Gospel of Jesus by working through Paul in performing miraculous signs;
2. be more confident that the Spirit will give power to their own witness concerning Jesus;
3. witness about Jesus more easily and readily as God provides opportunities.

Small-Group Discussion Helps

Day 1 • Acts 28:1–6

1. Paul was the kind of person who either was telling others what to do or participated in what was going on, as here where he gathers firewood (v. 3). He was an active, industrious, helpful person. Paul couldn't stand around and watch others labor while he did nothing. No work was too demeaning for him.

2. (a) The islanders assumed that Paul was a murderer who had escaped death from the sea. They assumed that fate or justice would catch up with him by means of the viper—that he would swell up or fall over dead. When we see people suffer misfortune or sickness, we may be tempted to suspect that they are being punished for some wrong or evil in their lives. We too often conclude that they deserve what they are getting. (b) *For personal reflection. Sharing optional.* As time and interest permit, allow one or more volunteers to share their response.

3. **Challenge question.** The fact that Paul suffered no ill effects from the viper (v. 6) is not a command for us to try the same. (a) Paul himself did not deliberately pick up the viper. (b) Obviously, no. (c) Jesus told the 72 followers He sent out to witness, "I have given you authority to trample on snakes and scorpions and to overcome all the power of the enemy; nothing will harm you" (Luke 10:19). That statement also is not a command but a reassuring promise that God would protect them. Furthermore, the statement was made specifically to the 72, not to us. Listed as it is with "all the power of the enemy," the text may well be referring to evil spirits; the enemy is Satan himself. (Unless someone brings it up, it's probably best not to get into a discussion of Mark 16:18 with its shaky textual foundation. If someone does mention that text, point out that we cannot base a teaching or practice on a passage of Scripture that may not be genuine. Even if the passage is genuine, it was fulfilled in the time of the apostles, and such signs may not be referring to believers of every age. Most groups who have handled poisonous snakes in their worship have had members die as a result of snakebite. Most important: Focusing on snake handling rather than the preaching of the Gospel is hardly the way to build Christian faith and life: "Faith comes from hearing the … word of Christ" [Romans 10:17].)

Day 2 • Acts 28:7–13

4. Luke is specific that Paul "after prayer" placed his hands on Publius's father and healed him (v. 8). (a) Paul did not immediately heal everywhere he went. God may have indicated when Paul should heal, or perhaps Paul prayed about whether he should and God let him know. (b) The healings on Malta were intended to be signs to support the Gospel, which Paul lived and spoke about, and to glorify God. The healings may also be viewed as one of the blessings of Jesus on their hospitality (Matthew 10:40–42).

5. God gave Paul a "thorn" in the flesh (2 Corinthians 12:7–9) in order to keep Paul humble and trusting in Him. The Lord knew that Paul's special revelations and visions from God might tempt him to think more highly of himself than he ought. Healings today may be for the good of the individual (Romans 8:28), to serve to spread the Gospel, to bring glory to God, or a combination of these. But for others God may have different purposes in mind, perhaps purposes like those He had for Paul's "thorn" in the flesh.

Day 3 • Acts 28:14–20

6. (a) God had promised Paul that he would get safely

to Rome (Acts 23:11) and now that the promise was fulfilled, Paul was thankful. (b) Paul had "wanted" to visit Rome for a long time, as indicated in his Letter to the Romans. Their faith had been reported all over the world. Paul looked forward to sharing some spiritual gift with them and to being mutually edified (Romans 1:8–12).

7. Jews were in the habit of calling other Jews "brothers" because they were of the same blood; together they were sons of Abraham. Christians called one another "brothers" whether they were Jews or Gentiles because they were one in the blood of Christ, members of the household of God.

8. Paul was allowed to live by himself, perhaps with his traveling companions, Aristarchus and Luke, and a group of soldiers to guard him, one on duty all the time (v. 16). Paul received guests and speaks about being "bound with this chain" (v. 20). It seems he means that he was chained to a guard. In Jerusalem the chains must have been shackles used for violent prisoners, but the chain in Rome a simple connection to his guard. In the letters Paul wrote from Rome he mentioned his chains. In Philippians 1:12–14 he tells us that the palace guard heard the Gospel and others were encouraged to speak boldly because of the chains. While the "chains" with which we have to contend may not be made of iron or steel, they can chafe and confine nonetheless. Still, like Paul, we can be confident that God can and does bring good out of bad.

9. (a) Paul tells the Jewish leaders that it was for the "hope of Israel" that he was bound with a chain (v. 20). The "hope of Israel" is the same reason Paul used in all his defenses. Before the Sanhedrin he said, "I stand on trial because of my hope in the resurrection of the dead" (Acts 23:6). Before Felix he identified the hope as the same as that of his accusers (Acts 24:15). Before Agrippa he says the hope was promised to the fathers (Acts 26:6–7). Thus, it includes all that the prophets had prophesied and that was fulfilled in the Christ: forgiveness of sin, life, and salvation through the risen Christ, the Messiah promised to Israel. (b) Seek a personal witness from participants, related to their hope in Jesus for His guidance in their future plans and everyday life, for the forgiveness of sins and eternal life they have in Him.

Day 4 • Acts 28:21–24

10. Listening to what another person believes is the best way to begin a witness conversation because it earns the right to share what you believe and helps you apply the Gospel to where that person is spiritually. If you first share an example of your own, others in your group may be encouraged to share.

11. Matthew's Gospel, reflecting the Jewish aversion to pronouncing the name of God, prefers to use the expression "kingdom of heaven" instead of "kingdom of God," but the same thing is meant. Jesus is the King. All authority was given to Him (Matthew 28:18). Paul calls Him King and even King of kings (1 Timothy 1:17; 6:15). Jesus taught His disciples to pray in the Lord's Prayer, "Thy kingdom come" (see Matthew 6:10). Encourage participants to say what they mean when they pray that God's kingdom would come. Such answers will probably refer to the way God rules in their own lives or to more people coming to believe the Gospel so that the church might grow.

12. The place where Paul stayed must have had a large meeting room, or perhaps they found a place outside to sit and talk. With half of the group who came returning at the end of the day as believers, this must have made a great impact on the large number of Jews in Rome, and it was only one day's work. Paul was going to be there for two years (v. 30)! No wonder God said that Paul must "testify in Rome" (Acts 23:11).

Day 5 • Acts 28:25–31

13. **Challenge question.** Paul quoted the same words of Isaiah 6:9–10 that Jesus did when His disciples asked Him why He spoke in parables (Matthew 13:14–15). The message was that the people have rejected the Lord, they will not understand, they can no longer believe. Isaiah said that the Jewish people had become calloused (v. 27). The word means their hearts were encased in thick fat and so could not be reached. Their ears and eyes were half shut, so they couldn't understand. If they did "understand" God would heal. God wants all people saved, but when they harden their hearts and reject Him, He finally rejects them.

14. (a) Romans 1:16: The Gospel is the power of God for salvation to everyone who believes, for the Jew first, then for the Gentile. (b) Romans 3:9, 23: Both Jews and Gentiles are under the power of sin and fall short of the glory of God. (c) Romans 3:24: All are justified by His grace as a gift. (d) Romans 10:12–13: There is no difference between Jew and Gentile. Everyone who calls on the name of the Lord will be saved and richly blessed.

15. (a) Paul told the Philippians that he was "confident" that he would "come soon" (Philippians 2:24). (b) He told Philemon at Colosse to prepare a guest room for him because "I hope" to be restored to you in answer to your prayers (Philemon 22). (c) Paul's plan, before it was interrupted by his arrest, was to visit Rome and go on from there to Spain (Romans 15:24, 28). The church historian Eusebius is one of the early writers who indicated that Paul took the Gospel to Spain.

16. Luke's purpose was to record how the Gospel spread from Jerusalem to Rome, and when he completed that purpose he ended his book. The book of the acts of the Holy Spirit continues to be written today as the disciples, including you and me, are His witnesses and carry the Gospel to the "ends of the earth" (Acts 1:8).

9780758600905